The
Bridesmaid
Guide

The Bridesmaid Guide

FULLY REVISED AND UPDATED

*Modern Advice on
Etiquette, Parties, and
Being Fabulous*

*

Kate Chynoweth

Illustrations by Neryl Walker

CHRONICLE BOOKS
SAN FRANCISCO

Library of Congress Cataloging-in-Publication Data

Chynoweth, Kate.

The bridesmaid guide : modern advice on etiquette, parties, and being fabulous / Kate Chynoweth.—Rev. and updated.

p. cm.

ISBN 978-1-4521-0240-5 (pbk.)

1. Bridesmaids. 2. Wedding etiquette. I. Title.

BJ2065.W43C48 2011

395.2'2—dc22

2011005872

Manufactured in China

Designed by Sugar

100 Layer Cake is a registered trademark of 100 Layer Cake Amanda Halbrook, Jillian Clark, Kristina Meltzer Partnership. Academy Awards is a registered trademark of Academy of Motion Picture Arts and Sciences Corp. Altoids is a registered trademark of Wm. Wrigley Jr. Co. American Idol is a registered trademark of FremantleMedia North America, Inc. Amnesty International is a registered trademark of Amnesty International of the U.S.A. Inc. Ann Taylor is a registered trademark of Annco, Inc. Anthropologie is a registered trademark of U.O. Merchandise, Inc. Astroglide is a registered trademark of Daniel X. Wray. Babeland is a registered trademark of Toys In Babeland. Band-Aid is a registered trademark of Johnson & Johnson Corp. Barbie is a registered trademark of Mattel, Inc. Beau-coup is a registered trademark of Beaucoup Wedding Favors, Inc. BHLDN is a registered trademark of Urban Outfitters, Inc. Birkenstock is a registered trademark of Birkenstock Orthopaedie GMBH & Co. Botox is a registered trademark of Allergan, Inc. Bumpits is a registered trademark of Big Happie Hair, Inc. BVD is a registered trademark of The B.V.D. Licensing Corp. Campari is a registered trademark of Davide Campari, Milano S.P.A. Craigslist is a registered trademark of craigslist, Inc. David's Bridal is a registered trademark of DBD, Inc. Doodle is a registered trademark of Doodle AG Société. Etsy is a registered trademark of Etsy, Inc. Evite is a registered trademark of Evite LLC. Expedia is a registered trademark of Expedia, Inc. Facebook is a registered trademark of Facebook, Inc. Flickr is a registered trademark of Yahoo! Inc. Glee is a registered trademark of Twentieth Century Fox Film Corp. Green Giant is a registered trademark of General Mills Marketing, Inc. Hooters is a registered trademark of HI Limited Partnership Hooters Enterprises, LLC. Hotwire is a registered trademark of Hotwire, Inc. J. Crew is a registered trademark of J. Crew Int'l, Inc. Kayak is a registered trademark of Kayak Software Corporation. The Knot is a registered trademark of The Knot, Inc. Magic 8 Ball is a registered trademark of Mattel, Inc. The Newlywed Game is a registered trademark of Columbia Tristar Television, Inc. Nintendo Wii is a registered trademark of Nintendo of America, Inc. Once Wed is a registered trademark of Once Wed Publishing, LLC. Orbitz is a registered trademark of Orbitz, LLC. Pantone is a registered trademark of Pantone LLC. Paper Source is a registered trademark of Paper Source, Inc. Paperless Post is a registered trademark of Paperless, Inc. Priceline is a registered trademark of Travelweb. Q-Tip is a registered trademark of Unilever Supply Chain, Inc. Sephora is a registered trademark of Sephora Corp. Shutterfly is a registered trademark of Shutterfly.com, Inc. Skype is a registered trademark of Skype Ltd. Corp. Southwest is a registered trademark of Southwest Airlines Co. Spanx is a registered trademark of Spanx, Inc. Style Me Pretty is a registered trademark of Style Me Pretty Abigail Larson. Swarovski is a registered trademark of Swarovski Aktiengesellschaft. Target is a registered trademark of Target Brands, Inc. Travelocity is a registered trademark of Travelocity .com LP. True Blood is a registered trademark of Home Box Office, Inc. Velcro is a registered trademark of Velcro Industries, B.V. Victoria's Secret is a registered trademark of Victoria's Secret Stores Brand Management, Inc. Weddingbee is a registered trademark of eHarmony, Inc. WeddingWire is a registered trademark of WeddingWire, Inc. The White Stripes is a registered trademark of John White and Megan White. Whitesnake is a registered trademark of Whitesnake Recorded Entertainment, Inc. Yelp is a registered trademark of Yelp! Inc. YouTube is a registered trademark of Google, Inc. Zappos is a registered trademark of Zappos IP, Inc. Zingerman's is a registered trademark of Dancing Sandwich Enterprises, Inc. Zipcar is a registered trademark of Zipcar, Inc.

10 9 8 7 6 5 4 3 2

Chronicle Books LLC
680 Second Street
San Francisco, California 94107
www.chroniclebooks.com

To the countless fabulous women who shared
with me their bridesmaid highs and lows: thank you!
Special appreciation goes to my agent, Ann Rittenberg, as
well as the Chronicle Books team who helped
this new edition come together, including Jodi Warshaw,
Laura Lee Mattingly, and designer Alison Oliver. A fresh
manuscript wouldn't have been possible without the
original, and for their inspiration and work the first
time around, gratitude goes to Mikyla Bruder and
Neryl Walker. For endless encouragement, a shout
out to my friends and family, especially Judy Chynoweth,
Gray and Tara Chynoweth, and my cousin, Christy
Ellinger, a paragon of manners and good taste.
Finally, thanks and love to my husband, Dave,
and our daughters, Lucy and June.

Table of Contents

✳ SECTION 4: THE BACHELORETTE PARTY

✳ SECTION 5: THE WEDDING WEEKEND

Introduction

IT'S MORE THAN HIGH TIME for a new edition of this book given the evolution of modern weddings. Since the original guide was published in 2002, all kinds of fresh challenges have cropped up for bridesmaids. Whether it's handling etiquette issues around electronic invitations and online photo sharing, or knowing which Web sites will help you plan a great party, technology is now as much a part of being a bridesmaid as taffeta and emotional tears.

Sharing all the tips bridesmaids need to stay savvy, along with key strategies for staying sane as brides' expectations for their weddings rise ever higher, is the goal of these pages. You'll find new text on modern etiquette and budgeting strategies throughout, with special attention paid to helpful Web sites; a resources section at the back highlights key online tools. Also, the text will direct you to downloadable invitations, shower games, and other stylish hostess helpers that are specially designed and inspired by this book, making your to-do list much lighter. Perhaps most important of all, you'll find updated hosting ideas and creative inspiration, so the pre-wedding parties that you host—which will only happen once in your best friend's lifetime, if all goes according to plan—are unforgettable.

Despite the changes technology has brought to the world of weddings, what never changes about being a bridesmaid is that it's ultimately about love and friendship. After all, a bridesmaid, at her most fabulous, transcends the role of practical helper to play an even more extraordinary role in the wedding: an unwavering bridge between the bride's old life and the new. As only a best friend can, she remembers the bride's biggest achievements and her most hilarious blunders, and she knows exactly how to celebrate her past and her future in style. Being a bridesmaid is about being there for the bride in your full mind, body, and spirit (preferably, with a full cocktail in your hand). It's about living in the moment and learning to laugh when you're wearing the worst dress of your life. Ultimately, being a bridesmaid is about finding special ways to celebrate friendship—and it provides the perfect excuse to party with the girls. Amen to that.

1

BEING FABULOUS

About Modern Weddings

Being a fabulous bridesmaid takes more work than it used to. After centuries of the same-old in regards to weddings, brides, and bridesmaids, more than a wee bit of change has crept in lately. Social networking, bridal blogs, wedding TV, online shopping for the full range of wedding gear, and the new immediacy that governs everything from posting photos to sending texts have transformed the way that brides do business. By default, the bridesmaid's role has transformed, too. That's why this book has been thoroughly revised and updated and includes a brand-new online resources section at the back—all devoted to helping you navigate the world of weddings today.

Fortunately, as being a bridesmaid becomes more high-tech, new Web tools have cropped up to make the job easier. Online scheduling sites that allow every bridesmaid to input her availability make it straightforward to find dates that work for showers and other events. Online shopping means you can view potential bridesmaid gowns and cast a vote for what you prefer or even design a dress by selecting its hem length or neckline. Whether your bridesmaid role is party planner, makeup expert, shopping maven, speechwriter, or scheduler extraordinaire, there's an ever-growing number of ways to get support online. Introducing Web sites that can help bridesmaids save money and time is part of the inspiration for this revised edition.

At the same time, the purpose of this book remains simple: to help you survive the bride's wedding madness with style and have fun while you're at it. As with friendship, love underlies the task of helping a dear friend get married, and at its core, this book is about preserving that—by giving you all the tools you need to stay positive, stay in touch, and above all, stay fabulous.

Golden Rules

The most important aspect of being a bridesmaid is finding that fun-loving attitude and bride-love within—so before we break down the etiquette and describe exactly what the job entails, you'll want to read up on these golden rules, the basic principles that every fabulous bridesmaid should live by.

BE FABULOUS

Being fabulous means being loyal, enthusiastic, fun, gorgeous, and true. It is about being the best friend you can be. This has everything to do with attitude—feeling love and respect for the bride—and little to do with money or perfect attendance at the pre-wedding parties. (If you don't love and respect her on some level, think again about being her bridesmaid: If you have doubts in the beginning, just imagine how you'll feel after you've spent hundreds of dollars, hosted parties, and logged hours giving moral support.) When your love for the bride is alive, pre-wedding magic is afoot. Fulfilling your duties will come naturally, and you'll have fabulous fun while you're at it!

STAY TECHNO SAVVY

In any job, staying on top of technology is essential, and being a bridesmaid is no different. Know which Web sites will help you better organize the shower or find a fantastic shopping deal (for great ideas, see Resources, page 140). Prioritize computer tasks; it only takes a few minutes to view a bridesmaid dress style online or research the cost of a flight to Vegas for a bachelorette party. Download the invitation and party game templates we've provided (go to www.chroniclebooks.com/bridesmaidguide).

KNOW THE BRIDE

Brides are as different from each other as snowflakes, and every bride will want different things from her bridesmaids. Use your knowledge of her personality to provide the kind of support she'll need. Does she have a particularly obnoxious mother-in-law? Run interference when the woman gets bossy. Is she concerned about finding the perfect gown? Tour the bridal boutiques by her side. As her friend, you have everything it takes to be the best bridesmaid around—especially if you are thoughtful enough to ask how you can help, instead of assuming you know her well enough to read her mind.

HAVE NO EXPECTATIONS

Getting married is overwhelming, and sometimes brides become neurotic versions of their former selves. Don't abandon her when she needs you most! Your emotional support and comic relief are the keys to her sanity. She may not be able to give back in the way she would under normal circumstances, but if you set aside your expectations—for example, that she should reward your efforts with formal thank-yous or gifts—you won't be disappointed. Cut her slack, often and always.

BOND, GIRL!

Whether or not you already know the other bridesmaids, bond with them. You are the bride's dear friends, and she wants you to get along. (Handing out copies of this book to all the maids is a wise contribution to wedding party harmony.) Having a tight-knit group of attendants is every bride's dream come true—see page 19 for fun team-building tips to make it happen.

TAKE DIRECTION

The bride is your director, and together you are putting on a fabulous show—even if the wedding ceremony is simply a few close friends and family members gathered in an open field. This means that, for the most part, you should chuck your own opinions out the window. No matter how knowledgeable you are about weddings, do not make assumptions about what the bride wants. Don't assume that she is going to choose wedding colors just because you, your sister, or your other friend did. Think about her. Is she the type to know—or care—about such formalities? If not, you should not try to press any tradition, no matter how important in your opinion, upon her.

FABULOUS TIP >>>>>→

HOW TO CREATE A SIGNATURE COCKTAIL

Signature cocktails are fixtures at weddings, but every fabulous bridesmaid knows they are equally welcome at bridal showers and bachelorette parties. To create yours, start with a wine or spirit like champagne or vodka that guests are familiar with. Use a basic formula with a twist—say, a martini made with cucumber vodka or a champagne cocktail flavored with pomegranate. Come up with a clever name for the drink that honors the bride or the couple or that just makes people laugh. If the drink has a lot of components make it ahead of time in pitchers for easier serving, and consider color: a rose-colored drink made with Campari or cranberry juice will beautifully complement a gift table adorned with pink and white details.

Official Duties

Behind every dazzling bride is an efficient crew of bridesmaids—the ladies who help the wedding love boat sail on smooth waters. All that's required is that you be your most fun, funny, and fabulous self and that you take charge of a few basic tasks. This practical list includes the essential duties every bridesmaid needs to do to nail her job with creativity and class. If you're the maid of honor, know that your fancy title and prestigious place near the altar does require a little extra—read on for your additional honors.

* Purchase the bridesmaid dress and shoes (without complaint), and be prepared to pay for professional makeup and hairstyling, unless you can adequately do your own.

* Be generous with your time and labor in the months before the wedding. Ask the bride if she would like your help with specific tasks, such as scouting for bridesmaids' dresses or stuffing invitations.

* Attend as many pre-wedding parties and events as possible.

* Help plan and cohost the wedding shower and bachelorette party. Contribute financially to these events, and go in on group gifts.

* Provide constant emotional support and maintain your sense of humor.

* Arrange for your transportation to and from the wedding, and pay for your accommodations if necessary. Just because you are part of the wedding party, do not expect the bride to reserve or pay for your room and ride—these expenses are on your shoulders.

* Budget your gift-giving funds. In addition to buying a wedding present, you will most likely also give her gifts at the engagement party, bridal shower, and bachelorette festivities. How much should you spend? From least to most: bachelorette party, engagement party, bridal shower, wedding.

* Keep a record of gifts received at the showers so the bride and groom can write thank-yous. Collect any gift envelopes brought to the reception and keep them in a safe place.

* The day of the ceremony, be there for the bride. Don't sneak off at any point, no matter how much you want

to steal a private moment with the photographer's gorgeous assistant. The bride might need you.

* Attend the rehearsal dinner and ceremony. Stand in the receiving line after the wedding at the bride's request.

* Act as an auxiliary hostess at the reception by introducing people, directing them to the bar, or helping them find their table—but only if it seems necessary.

* Hit the dance floor with butt-shaking enthusiasm when the time comes, even if nobody else is dancing. Don't be afraid that you'll make a fool of yourself. Dance with your designated usher if necessary—but in that situation, keep the butt shaking to a minimum.

* Be prepared to give a toast (or roast) at the rehearsal dinner or wedding. Technically, this is a maid of honor duty, but there are many occasions when it may be necessary, or just plain fun, for a bridesmaid or the whole bridal party to do the honors.

MAID OF HONOR: EXTRA DUTIES

* Attend one of the wedding dress fittings with the bride.

* Make sure that all the bridesmaids have their dresses and accessories, that their hair and makeup is taken care of, that they get to the ceremony on time, and that they have the correct bouquets.

* Arrange the bride's train and veil before the ceremony begins and just after she arrives at the altar. Be prepared to help her "bustle the train" before the dancing begins. (This is why you have to go to the fittings—so you can learn the art of removing or shortening the train.)

* Hold the groom's wedding ring during the ceremony.

* Hold the bouquet while the couple exchanges rings and vows.

* Along with the best man, sign the wedding certificate as a legal witness.

* Stand in the receiving line, if necessary. Dance with the best man during the formal first-dance sequence. Also, dance with the groomsmen or anyone else who looks lonely for a partner.

* Help the bride change for her honeymoon if she's leaving right away, and take charge of her gown until she returns.

* Wrap up the reception, literally. At the end of the evening, make sure the top tier of the cake has been preserved as the bride directed, and fill a small bag or box with reception items such as the cake topper, menu, printed matchbook, or program. You may even offer to help the mother of the bride, who usually handles any incoming gifts. Your thoughtfulness on all fronts will be noticed and appreciated.

Online Helpline

These days, the Internet is every bride's best friend. But guess what? The online tools brides use to plan weddings can also be a huge help to bridesmaids. Read on and take advantage.

WEDDING WEB SITES

Need to Know: Launching a wedding Web site devoted exclusively to the nuptials is nearly as common these days as sending a save-the-date card. Ideally, the site design makes it easy for guests to take care of essentials like reserving a hotel room or finding the couple's registry. It might be a single page with a bare minimum of detail or a sprawling multipage site that includes everything from dining, child care, and recreational options to—yes, you guessed it—bios and photos of the wedding attendants.

Bridesmaid Benefit: Whether you can't remember the start time of the rehearsal dinner or you need a quick link to gift ideas, these sites are a major help when it comes to practical planning. Plus, if the site includes photos of the attendants, you can scope out the groomsmen.

THE WORD ALERT: *ENCORE WEDDING*

More than 40 percent of weddings held today are what's known as "encore" weddings, where the bride, the groom, or both, have been married before. Increasingly, remarrying couples will involve children in the bridal party. But that doesn't mean close friends are off the hook— it just means you might be wearing the same bridesmaid dress as a twelve-year-old. Good luck! ✳**USAGE:** The bride's mother says, *"Please don't call it Julie's second marriage. Call it her encore wedding."*

BRIDAL BLOGS

Need to Know: Popular sites like Weddingbee (www.weddingbee.com), Once Wed (www.oncewed.com), Style Me Pretty (www.stylemepretty.com), and 100 Layer Cake (www.100layercake.com) have joined long-established online resources such as The Knot (www.theknot.com) in providing brides with a bottomless source of information, from wedding planning lists and ideas to vendor guides, DIY projects, and fashion look books, plus stories and photos of real weddings.

Bridesmaid Benefit: If the bride is really keeping up with her blogs, she should be exposed to all the latest trends for bridesmaids—among the biggest of which is (a) allowing the maids to choose the price range for the dress and (b) selecting styles that are flattering and can be worn again and again. If she seems clueless, send her a link to one and suggest how much fun you had reading it. Also, look around for ideas. Great shower themes and stories from successful bridesmaid-hosted showers are often posted.

MESSAGE BOARDS

Need to Know: Message boards (also sometimes called forums) provide an online space where brides can rant about everything from dress shops to, yes, their bridesmaids and the maid of honor. Larger sites such as Weddingbee and The Knot host the most garrulous and diverse boards. Search functions make it easy to search previous posts. (You didn't think you were the only bridesmaid in the world being asked to wear a cowboy hat, did you?)

Bridesmaid Benefit: Nobody wants to tell a bride directly if she's about to transgress the boundaries of good taste, which puts you in an awkward position when it comes to giving advice. If she needs guidance you feel uncomfortable giving, suggest that she post to the boards and find out how other brides have handled similar problems. This might be like sending Alice down the rabbit hole. Or she might love the online bridal community so much that she adopts its lingo as her own. If so, here are a few key translations: FI (Fiancé); DH (Dear Husband); MOB (Mother of the Bride); FMIL (Future Mother-in-Law); WR (Wedding Related); BP (Bridal Party); and last, but not most flatteringly, BM (Bridesmaid).

SOCIAL NETWORKING SITES

Need to Know: Sites like Facebook, where friends—and often work colleagues and extended family—share information, photos, and personal details, make it easier than ever to keep track of a far-flung network of peers. When it comes to weddings, however, they can be a venue for inadvertently offending someone, excluding them, or stealing their thunder. (From this file: the afternoon the bride calls you sobbing because the groom posted their engagement online before she could call her sister with the news.)

Bridesmaid Benefit: There's an easy rule of thumb here: Don't post anything related to the bridal shower, bachelorette party, or wedding, whether it's news, specific event details, or photos, unless the bride asks you to do so. Or, if you're dying to post, ask the bride first.

Bridesmaid Bonding

When the bridal party is a tight group of friends who live in the same city, bonding happens naturally. When the bridesmaids hail from different parts of the country, however, breaking the ice is an essential first step toward making the pre-wedding festivities and gift giving go off without a hitch. You don't have to wait for the bride or the maid of honor to formally introduce you—any bridesmaid can seize the bull by the horns. Use these tried-and-true techniques for getting the girls to bond.

REACH OUT

A note is a great way to break the ice. Get the e-mail addresses of the bridal party members from the bride and introduce yourself. Include a few fun personal details (astrological sign, occupation, favorite cocktail), list your contact information, and reference the bride to remind everyone that she is the common denominator. (For example, if she has a reputation for being wild at parties, say something like, "Why do I have the feeling she'll out-party us all?") Encourage the bridesmaids to introduce themselves in a similar fashion by responding to your note. In some cases, the bride may do this footwork for you by setting up, for example, a Facebook group where all the girls can connect. But if she doesn't, e-mail is a great option that offers privacy.

CHOOSE DATES ONLINE

Choosing a time for a bridal shower or bachelorette party can quickly become a nightmare of "reply all" e-mails as various bridesmaids overshare about why the suggested dates are impossible. Instead, be the smart one and use Doodle (www.doodle.com), a free scheduling Web site where you follow easy steps to create a calendar of potential dates and then ask key players to vote on what works.

BUDDY UP

Two is better than one when it comes to bridesmaids. Whether the task is planning the menu for the shower or buying some hot lingerie for the bride's bachelorette gift, chores are more fun done in tandem—and you and your partner might just become dear friends. Splitting into dynamic duos can also lighten the load of attending multiple fittings or appointments with the bride; send one pair to the first event, another to the second. If you don't feel comfortable assigning yourself a partner, ask the maid of honor to take charge of pairing you up to tackle certain tasks.

GET PERSONAL

Collaborate on a personal and creative gift for the bride—it doesn't have to be anything expensive! Have the group write an irreverent song or poem dedicated to her. Get the ball rolling by writing the first segment yourself, circulating it via e-mail, and suggesting that the others contribute a creative line as well. You might also create a scrapbook, which could be sent sequentially to the bridesmaids, each of whom could contribute a story, anecdote, poem, or drawing before mailing it on to the next attendant on the list. (Allow a couple of weeks for mailing time.) Making a digital photo book online that celebrates the bride's timeline of friendships with the bridesmaids is another way to create a prized memento.

Handling Common Challenges

It's common for a bridesmaid to run into a challenge or two during her tour of duty—but even the most awkward situations can be resolved with honesty and tact. Whether the problem is flying across the country twice (for the bridal shower and the wedding), or being asked to cover a beloved tattoo revealed by a spaghetti-strap dress, these tips will help you navigate the most common rough spots with ease.

CHALLENGE: SURVIVING LONG DISTANCE

• *Get face time.* Use Skype or video chat to stay in touch. Seeing each other makes everything more fun—and as you model the bridesmaid dress for her, or she shows you her wedding shoes, or you just share giggles over a glass of wine, you'll prove that your friendship can go the distance.

• *Take initiative.* The bride may be too busy to call you, so be sure to reach out (maybe even build a couple of reminders into your monthly calendar). Frequent no-pressure check-ins, even just a one-line text message, will let her know she's on your mind and give her a chance to vent if she needs it.

• *Offer perspective.* If you're a maid of honor in California and the bride is in Connecticut, you may occasionally feel out of the loop as local bridesmaids fill in for you at dress fittings and other appointments. But worry not. Many brides treasure having an out-of-towner to talk to, someone who is far away from the hustle and bustle of their family and wedding details and who can provide a sense of humor and distanced perspective on the event.

• *Manage expectations.* If you are an out-of-town bridesmaid and know you can't afford to fly to a shower or bachelorette party in addition to the wedding, tell the bride in advance. If she is really your friend, she won't begrudge your staying on budget.

• *Be generous.* You may be asked by the maid of honor or other bridesmaids to contribute to the cost of the shower or bachelorette party even if you cannot attend. Etiquette does not require that you comply with the request, but if you can afford it, helping to foot the bill is a very generous gesture. Other ways to participate appropriately include sending a shower gift, planning a separate celebration with the bride when you do arrive in town, sending flowers, or contributing to a group gift.

• *Fly early.* A bride's schedule is often tight in the days preceding her wedding, but if she likes the idea, you could fly in a few days before the final twenty-four-hour countdown begins. Doing something special together, whether it's a group spa day with all the bridesmaids or a luncheon with just the two of you, is sure to be fun. You can also offer to help her with any prep work that still needs to be done.

CHALLENGE: TWO MAIDS OF HONOR

Who doesn't know the old adage "two heads are better than one"? The practice of having two maids of honor is becoming more common, either because the bride wants both her sister and her best friend to stand up with her, or because she has two fabulous friends she cannot choose between. When this is the case, the two maids of honor split the tasks between them. If there is a particular duty you were looking forward to—holding the ring or signing the marriage license, for example—speak with the bride early on, and be flexible, of course. Otherwise, pair up with your wedding coworker to tackle challenging tasks like planning and hosting the shower or scripting a spectacular speech. The maid of honor who lives closer to the bride may take on the more practical duties, such as hosting a shower or party, but both can equally share the financial, emotional, and practical obligations. Good communication is the key to avoiding tussles over this post's considerable duties.

CHALLENGE: BRIDESMAN OR GROOMSMAID

Some brides may include a fabulous male friend (bridesman) in the wedding party. His attire will likely be a suit or tux, perhaps with a vest or tie that matches the bridesmaid dresses; his duties are essentially the same as those of any other bridesmaid, offering support and being part of the pro-bride team. So where's the challenge? Well, it's not always obvious how to handle his role in pre-wedding events. Does the bride want him invited to the otherwise all-female shower or bachelorette party? If not, does she expect him to help organize it anyway? With such questions on the table, the best idea is to check in with the bride so her wishes are honored. Ditto if the wedding includes a groomsmaid, a female friend or relative who is part of the groom's entourage and will stand with the groomsmen—the bride may wish to invite her to some of the all-girl pre-wedding events.

CHALLENGE: PREGNANT, TATTOOED, OR PURPLE-HAIRED BRIDESMAID

A pregnant bridesmaid was once considered to be in poor taste, but thankfully those days are over! Today, the bridesmaid's relationship to the bride, not her personal situation, is the pertinent matter, and the only real concern should be whether or not the pregnant bridesmaid will be physically comfortable standing for the ceremony. (If you are pregnant and want the post, reassure the bride that you are looking forward to it so she doesn't fret that she's asking too much of you.) Most brides will be flexible around other appearance-related issues, too. But if she asks you to modify your hair color or cover a beloved tattoo, only do so if you feel perfectly comfortable with the change. If not, and the bride insists on having her way, gracefully explain that this is a deal-breaker for you—ideally, when presented with the prospect of losing you as a bridesmaid, she will think twice about her request. Although the bride's wishes should generally come first around her wedding, friendship is a two-way street, and all interactions should be marked by mutual respect.

Bridesmaid Blunders to Avoid

The road to hell is paved with good intentions, as they say, and that is truer for bridesmaids than for almost anyone else. Even when she has the bride's best interest at heart, a bridesmaid can overstep her bounds and unwittingly torment the bride. The worst part is that the bride may be too polite to mention the problem, in which case the poor bridesmaid will never know her error or understand why the bride seems slightly hostile. For the record, here is a list of the most common mistakes to avoid.

REPEATEDLY ASKING THE BRIDE ABOUT WEDDING DETAILS

You might think you're being thoughtful by asking the bride if she has chosen her "colors," sent out her invitations, selected the caterer, or completed other tasks—but, in all likelihood, you are tormenting her by reminding her of issues she has yet to resolve. If you must inquire, be sure you ask only once. She will bring her problems to you, if she wants to talk about them. (The fact that you did everything in a timely and orderly fashion is no reason to harass her.) Your job isn't to talk about the wedding; it's the opposite! Remind her that it's a big world out there, with lots of ridiculous things in it: Tell her about the thong-sporting Betty you saw at the gym who fell off of her treadmill, or how you smiled at that cute guy and later realized you had poppy seeds in your teeth. Whatever you do, don't take your job so seriously that you start pressuring the bride. That's what wedding planners, mothers, and in-laws are for.

POSTING WEDDING-RELATED PHOTOS OR COMMENTS ON THE WEB

Social networking has accustomed many of us to posting photos of and comments about events as they happen or immediately afterward— but when it comes to pre-wedding events and the nuptials themselves, discretion is essential. Even if you played shutterbug at the bridal shower, don't post photos before asking the bride's permission. She may want to avoid a situation where people who weren't invited could view the images and feel excluded or upset. As for photos of the wedding itself? First of all, you should avoid taking pictures during the ceremony—leave it to the professionals. That said, if you have a few reception photos that are irresistibly cute, it should be okay to share the joy (unless, of course, an image is somehow compromising or potentially embarrassing). Always ask first. Reconsider if your bride is very type A and controlling about her image; if this is the case, skip posting anything, ever.

CONSTANTLY TALKING ABOUT YOUR WEDDING OUTFIT

Some brides will want you to look just so—and you'll know when this is the case, because she'll prescribe not just the dress and shoes, but your hair, makeup, accessories, and possibly even lingerie. Other brides will choose the basics and leave the rest to you, which means that she doesn't really care what lipstick shade, stocking hue, or hairstyle you select. Whatever breed of bride you've got, take the advice she gives and go with it, and if you need to consult someone, call a friend—one who isn't getting married. The bride has a thousand decisions to make, and she shouldn't have to mull over a thousand more with you.

EXPRESSING DOUBTS ABOUT THE GROOM

Whether you mention that he isn't handling the caterer very well, or get down to brass tacks and say you don't respect him, saying anything disparaging about the groom is the cardinal sin of bridesmaid-hood. Yet the number of bridesmaids who make negative comments about the groom is shocking. The bachelorette party is the only time when you might mention one of his slightly galling traits, couched as good-natured ribbing—but only to provide contrast with his good looks, talents, smarts, and skills.

EXPECTING A THANK-YOU

You've worked hard throwing all the parties, and the bride hasn't breathed a word of thanks. What should you do? Get over it. Move past your own hurt feelings. The truth is, many brides are too overwhelmed in the moment to notice how hard you're working. She'll shower you with love later, when her head gets screwed back on—remember this whenever her self-absorption is shaking your faith in the friendship. She loves you, you love her, you're both fabulous, and there's nothing to worry about!

Creativity Rules (What Can You Do for the Bride besides Throw Parties?)

If the couple in question loves to buck tradition, or if they are paying for their own wedding (on a shoestring), your role as bridesmaid or maid of honor can take an intriguing turn. As a bridesmaid, you follow the bride's lead—and if she's a free spirit, you'll have carte blanche to be creative. Here's your chance to do more than throw bridal showers and bachelorette parties!

SHOWCASE YOUR SKILLS

One of the most helpful things you can do is offer to take over some of the exorbitant but practical tasks that make weddings so profitable for caterers, florists, photographers, and stylists. Focus on your strengths. Do not, for example, offer to style her hair if you used to botch the job on your Barbie—but if you spent six months in cooking school, you might be the perfect person to bake her wedding cake.

PERFORM THE MARRIAGE CEREMONY

If the bride and groom aren't particularly religious and are planning a fun, freewheeling, and very casual ceremony, you can offer to be their officiant! Although the laws governing who can perform a legal marriage vary from state to state, in many places, filling out the appropriate paperwork is all it takes for you to marry your friends. The state marriage licensing bureau is the best place to ask for information; just be sure to get the wedding date right when you're completing the forms—your legal officiant status usually only lasts for twenty-four hours. Alternatively, check for Web sites where anyone willing to fill out a quick form online can become a legally ordained minister—interfaith and nondenominational, of course. Be sure the state where the wedding will take place recognizes the type of officiant license you obtain, as the marriage must be legal to be binding.

Many couples adore taking this off-the-beaten path to the altar, since having a dear friend conduct the ceremony can bring an intimacy that would otherwise be hard to achieve, especially with a justice of the peace or religious official who is a stranger to the bride and groom officiating at the wedding. If the couple choose to have you officiate, wear something that differs from the attire of the bride and groom and wedding party, although formal robes or vestments are certainly not required.

MAKE A MEDIEVAL HERBAL BRIDAL BOUQUET

Leave boring roses to the rest of the world, and make her an old-fashioned and unforgettable herbal bouquet to carry down the aisle. Select a variety of gorgeous fresh herbs, such as lavender, rosemary in bloom, and flowering oregano—for a June wedding, these should be seasonal and easy to find—and surround the herbs with sweet-smelling peonies, preferably in pale lavender or other pastels. Wrap them with a sage-colored ribbon, and anchor all the stems firmly to create a bouquet sturdy enough to survive the bridal toss. (If you aren't sure about your bouquet-wrapping or flower-arranging skills, go to a florist with the herbs in hand and ask them to finesse the rest.)

DO THE BRIDE'S WEDDING DAY MAKEUP

If the bride is a close friend, the wedding is very casual, and you are a decent hand with a powder brush, you may offer to do her makeup. (Don't be offended if she opts for professionals instead!) Budget plenty of time and energy for doing the job if she accepts your offer—finding the right look will definitely take more than a quick trip to the drugstore. After all, you want to do it right!

✳ **Step One:** Several weeks before the wedding, book an appointment for a free consultation at a makeup boutique like Sephora or a posh department store makeup counter. Do a little research and aim for products that fit the bride's budget—some lines are vastly more affordable than others. Bring a camera so you can take digital pictures of each "look" for later consideration. If you want to bring some fresh ideas of your own to the table, check out online makeup tutorials on anything from a smoky eye to a strong lip.

✳ **Step Two:** Go with the bride to the makeup appointment, and watch the consultant like a hawk—if the products and techniques are making her look like something from *The Rocky Horror Picture Show*, drag her out of there. Never lose sight of the fact that you are in charge of quality control. Encourage her not to stray too far from her normal look. Resist consultants who give you the hard sell.

✳ **Step Three:** Book another appointment at another location. Continue this pattern until you find a consultant who does a reasonably good job of turning your dear friend into a blushing bride. Take careful note of the consultant's techniques. Professionals often use special tricks to create a certain look—tricks that amateur cosmeticians might not know about.

✳ **Step Four:** Once the bride makes her final color and item selections—with your gentle guidance—she should purchase the makeup, just as she would if she had hired a professional. (Note: if you find the perfect lipstick during this process, you should pay for that separately. Every bridesmaid is financially responsible for her own hair and makeup, in addition to her dress and shoes, unless the bride suggests otherwise.)

✳ **Step Five:** Do several test runs. Try the products on the bride for reactions or allergies. Look at the results of your makeover in the same light as that in which the ceremony will occur—in direct sunlight if the wedding will be held outside in the afternoon, and so on. If she doesn't like the look you've created, don't take it personally—just try again. On the day of the wedding, do everything exactly as you did in your rehearsals. Voilà!

2

BRIDESMAIDS' NUTS AND BOLTS

Golden Rules

As much as weddings are about fun, there are nuts-and-bolts issues that every bridesmaid must face. Creating a budget, staying on top of a schedule, being savvy about etiquette, and dealing with the dress situation are just a few. Designed to familiarize you with the essentials of your new role, this section provides the bedrock foundation of knowledge you will need in order to survive—and thrive—as a bridesmaid. But first, take these golden rules to heart, and you'll manage to have fun even when the nitty-gritty detail work is at hand.

BE A BUDGET BRIDESMAID

The Budget Bridesmaid feels righteous and good about celebrating a beloved friend's happiness, even if it means dropping some cash. At the same time, she cuts corners and shops for bargains whenever possible, and she has a clear idea about her spending parameters. Remember: Effective cost cutting does not make you a cheap person or a bad friend. It means that you are thoughtful, and that you aren't willing to let money-related matters jeopardize your friendship with the bride.

MAKE ETIQUETTE LOOK EASY

Being well-mannered is not about following stiff conventions—it's about being charming and appropriate in every situation. Alas, in the world of today's weddings, etiquette is a moving target. Is it okay to e-mail the invites for the casual bachelorette party you're planning? Definitely. What about a formal shower to which the bride's grandmother and her friends are invited? Not so much. When in doubt, look to this book for guidance.

SAY YES TO YOUR DRESS

This section includes all kind of great tips for helping you look great in your dress, including a guide to your best undergarments and strategies for fittings. But keep this in mind: The simplest survival strategy for dealing with an unflattering bridesmaid dress is to graciously accept it. Wear whatever and pay whatever the bride requests, and keep your trap shut. Being in her wedding is more important to you than looking good.

BE GOOD TO YOURSELF

Part of being fabulous is being true, and this means being true to yourself. Don't sacrifice anything too dear for the bride and her wedding, or you might end up resentful. Be realistic about your schedule. If you don't live nearby and can't fly out for the shower, the bachelorette party, and the wedding, tell her in advance. Also, don't get caught up in petty drama with other bridesmaids. Remember the big picture: You love the bride, she loves you, and weddings are celebrations of love and friendship.

RSVP Etiquette

It's not every day that a beautifully designed wedding invitation arrives in your mailbox—when it does, you'll need to respond with grace and tact. Even if the bride has already asked you to be her bridesmaid and you have given your verbal consent, you should send the response card as soon as possible. Of course, with the increasing popularity of online RSVPs, you might find yourself at the keyboard instead of the writing desk. Read on for key pointers.

RSVP FOR YOUR GUEST

If the invitation is addressed to you and your significant other, you will RSVP for you both. However, being a bridesmaid does not automatically entitle you to bring a date. If the envelope has your name only, the implication is that you will fly solo. Venue seating capacities and overall expense can make it very difficult for couples to give everyone a "plus one." Asking for permission to bring someone after the invitation arrives is a no-no. One possible exception to this rule: You just got engaged or you are in a serious relationship the bride isn't aware of. Alternatively, if you're an extremely good friend of the bride and know the wedding budget isn't tight, you may bring up the issue with her—but it's not quite proper and you'll do so at your own risk. Terrible awkwardness may ensue. Bringing someone you have not RSVP'd for to the wedding is quite obviously not an option.

RSVP CARD

Many wedding invitations include a response card and stamped return envelope. Send your reply as soon as possible, giving all the information required. A quick response minimizes the chance you'll misplace the card (you wouldn't be the first). Don't include unnecessary details in your response, like the fact that you think your boyfriend is coming if he can cancel his business trip, or that you want to RSVP for a tall, handsome man but you haven't met him yet. Just stick with the script—especially because the cards might be opened by the bride's mother, sister, or in-laws who are assisting her with the guest list.

RSVP ONLINE

The vast majority of couples still stick to tradition and send paper wedding invitations by post. However, an engraved RSVP card that guests are supposed to mail back is no longer always included. Instead, it's increasingly common to ask guests to RSVP electronically. The option is reliable, saves money, prevents the hassle of manual counting (the computer automatically updates the number of responses, not to mention meal choices), and ensures nothing is misplaced in the mail. It's also environmentally friendly. The RSVP might be handled on the couple's wedding Web site or at a separate site that handles RSVPs exclusively. The details of how to proceed may be printed on the back of the paper invitation or printed on a separate engraved card that says something like "Please reply to www.foreverinlove.com before the first of December." Once you locate the Web site, you should be finished in a few clicks. If you're concerned about a technological glitch, you can always confirm your RSVP with the couple directly.

RSVP BY HAND

If a wedding invitation does not include an engraved card or online instructions, but simply says RSVP, you may write a response on your own stationery, in your own hand. While this is certainly old-fashioned, it's not unheard of. Plus, knowing how to write a well-mannered reply to a formal invitation is a charming skill that's worth acquiring. Your handwritten reply should include an abbreviated version of the invitation text and begin with your own name (and include that of your significant other, if he or she was invited):

Sarah Putman and Sean Clegg

accept with pleasure

the kind invitation of

Mr. and Mrs. Miller

for Saturday, the twenty-sixth of June

at six o'clock

Wilshire Ebell Women's Club

Your Budget and Smart Savings

Beware of hidden expenses! In the pre-wedding whirlwind of bridal showers, dress shopping, and parties, even the most budget-savvy bridesmaids can overspend by mistake. Because the events span several months or more, it can be easy to lose track of the big picture and splurge at each event. The figures listed here will give you a ballpark idea of the financial burden that has fallen on your lovely little shoulders.

THE DRESS (AND ALTERATIONS): $150–$600

Cha-ching! The dress is the big-deal item for every Budget Bridesmaid. In general, the dress cost will average around $150 to $200. If the bride insists on something more spendy, you have little choice but to pony up. Don't forget that the cost of alterations, which can be upward of a hundred bucks, can increase the overall price considerably. If the overall cost is a deal-breaker for you, address the situation with honesty and tact (don't resign without explanation). You could explain, for example, that you budgeted $200 for the dress and feel uncertain how to proceed given the more costly option at hand. Just know that while communicating your limited financial situation to the bride in the early stages is okay, she may exclude you from the wedding party as a result. More generous brides might choose a less expensive gown or even offer to pay for it. If she foots the bill for your dress, bring the secret to the grave, so that the other bridesmaids don't feel slighted.

Smart Savings

* Retailers that sell lines of bridesmaid dresses, like J. Crew, often offer deeply discounted prices on their Web sites. Savvy brides will know about this option, but if yours seems unaware, a tactful query as to whether she has scoped the Web for deals might not go amiss. Keep it light. If she seems disinterested in the tip, don't mention it again—but give yourself a gold star for being budget savvy.

* If the bride wants you to pay to have your hair and makeup professionally done on the day of the wedding, it is perfectly acceptable to ask her in advance if you can do your own beauty routine instead. If you will also have costly travel and lodging expenses, she shouldn't mind your cutting corners in order to afford the dress, especially if she has chosen something on the high end.

* If you are lucky enough to be allowed to select your own dress, look everywhere from bargain basements to department store sale racks to your close friends' closets. (Nobody has to know where you found the dress, or what you spent, besides you.) If you buy something brand-new, make sure it's returnable, in case the bride disagrees with your choice.

* When you purchase the dress or anything else online, try your best to score free shipping. If purchases over $250 ship without charge, for example, organize a group buy and have everything sent to one bridesmaid at no cost.

SHOES AND LINGERIE: $75–$250

We all live for fabulous shoes—and fabulous lingerie, for that matter—but when you need to cut costs, these are good places to skimp. Think twice about investing in pricey heels or bra and hose, unless special underwear is absolutely necessary to make you look and feel good in the dress. When it comes to shoes, consider bargain-basement options before purchasing something expensive.

Smart Savings

* Hit online retailers like Zappos (www.zappos.com), department store sale racks, or affordable chain stores. If you've been asked to wear dyed pumps and you already have some from another wedding, you can redye them if the color is darker.

* Go for the cheap stick-on cups instead of an expensive strapless bra (yes, they even come in sizes for chesty gals).

* Borrow that tummy-tucking thing from a good friend who shares your size.

* Go braless. Opt for inexpensive nipple covers (also known as breast petals or pasties) lest a chilly breeze turns you into the unexpected star of the show.

HAIR, MAKEUP, AND ACCESSORIES: $50–$350

The wide price range here accounts for the fact that the bride might want you to have your hair and makeup professionally done, which would obviously put you on the spendy end. Even if this is not required, however, you may still shell out for wedding day baubles and makeup, not to mention a manicure and pedicure. Sometimes, the bride asks all the bridesmaids to purchase matching accessories, in which case your hands are tied.

Smart Savings

* Many brides give bridesmaids matching jewelry to be worn at the wedding, so if the bride doesn't give specific requirements, don't invest in new jewels—you may get some the day of the wedding. Bring backup baubles along, just in case the bride doesn't give jewelry.

* With jewelry, less is more if the bride doesn't give a mandate. Don't be afraid to go bare, bargain-shop for accessories, or borrow your mother's pearls. Everyone will be too busy swooning over the bride to notice the details of your outfit.

* If she is not asking you to go the professional route, do your own hair, makeup, manicure, and pedicure.

TRANSPORTATION AND LODGING: $200–$1,000+

If you have to travel by plane, forget what you've heard about the dress being the most expensive item in the budget: When you add up the price of the plane ticket (or tickets, if you have to fly out once for the shower and once for the wedding) and accommodations, this cost definitely wins the prize as budget crasher. You are also responsible for arranging your own transportation from the airport to the wedding site, unless the bride offers you a ride.

Smart Savings

* Shop around for plane fares at a comprehensive travel site like Kayak (www.kayak.com). Or consider booking through a deep-discount provider like Hotwire (www.hot wire.com). The downside? You won't learn trip details such as the number of stops, exact times, and airline carrier information until you've already purchased the nonrefundable fare—which means you might have to fly a day early to make sure you won't miss the rehearsal dinner.

* Often, the bride and groom reserve a block of rooms at a group rate at a hotel located near the wedding site; call early to take advantage of the deal (if the rooms are booked by the time you call, you'll likely pay full price). If you are on your own, plan ahead and check out hotels online through the usual suspects including Hotwire and Priceline (www.priceline.com). The prices are bound to be better than what the front desk will give you at the last minute.

* Team up with other single bridesmaids and share a hotel room—but do not let the midnight munchies persuade you to devour those expensive minibar snacks!

* If the wedding is in an area where house rentals are available, research the cost and see if you can drum up enough people to share a place. Always keeping an eye out for personal safety and potential fraud issues, check out apartment-swap Web sites or the vacation rentals section of craigslist (craigslist.org), which can be great resources for finding affordable places to stay.

* If the bride has a friend who will put you up, consider it a good way to bond with someone new—and save some cash while you're at it.

* Avoid having to rent a car by teaming up with local bridesmaids. If you must rent, try to coordinate with someone else, so the entire cost doesn't fall on your shoulders. When there's no choice but to rent a car yourself, do some comparison shopping online. Certain airlines such as Southwest (www.southwest .com) sometimes offer good car-rental deals, as do discount providers like Hotwire and Priceline. For an alternative to traditional rentals, check out car-share companies like Zipcar (www.zipcar. com), which give you access to wheels in many urban areas.

A WEDDING GIFT TO THE COUPLE: $50–$200

As a bridesmaid, you may already be in the red—and not just that scarlet strapless bridesmaid number, either—by the time the wedding day arrives. Luckily, etiquette is on your side: You have an entire year from the date of the ceremony to send the couple a gift, and delaying the purchase might give your bank balance a chance to bounce back. The fact that you are part of the wedding party does not mean your gift has to be lavish or expensive. Since you know the bride so well, you may bypass the registry and offer her something unique, something you've made yourself, for example—but don't feel compelled to do this. Buying from the registry is absolutely fine. Essentially, this gift is at your discretion.

Smart Savings

* Couples usually create registries well in advance of their weddings, which gives you time to watch for deals. White sales or discounts on china collections that take place during the year can offer great savings. Or, if you happen to see an item the couple registered for at a better price somewhere else, go ahead and grab it—just remember to call the registry and have the item removed so they don't receive more than one.

* Use Etsy (www.etsy.com) as a resource to find reasonably priced one-of-a-kind gifts or commissioned items, from a whimsical portrait of the couple to river rocks engraved with love birds and their initials.

* Go in with others on a truly fabulous gift. This can work especially well if the couple has a honeymoon registry. Chip in with others to buy them two nights at their dream hotel on Capri or something equally luxurious. Just be sure to organize this effort with people you know, and arrange the finances in advance, so you don't have to chase anyone down for money after the fact.

* Get crafty. Whether your talent is for painting, sewing, photography, or ceramics, use your skills to make her something priceless.

THE SHOWER (INCLUDING GIFT): $50–$200

These days, it is common and perfectly acceptable for the maid of honor—who traditionally was responsible for footing the entire bill alone—to divide the financial burden among herself and the bridesmaids. Since none of the other guests at the shower should be asked for contributions, a long guest list might mean a large contribution from you. And, even if you help host, you should still bring a gift.

Smart Savings

✳ Use our adorable (and free!) invitation templates to craft the cards and shower games yourself instead of buying them (www.chroniclebooks.com/bridesmaidguide).

✳ Remember that shower gifts may be small. Elegant napkins, glassware, or other small household items are in keeping with the traditional intimate and tasteful shower, which these days is too frequently abandoned for a large party with lavish gifts.

✳ If you are attending more than one shower, you may elect to send the bride one significant item rather than bringing a less expensive one to every shower.

✳ If all the bridesmaids are splitting the cost, try to get on the planning committee and offer a voice of reason if the budget seems to be skyrocketing. (Ditto for the bachelorette party.)

✳ If you live far away and can't afford to fly out for the shower, you may gracefully decline the invitation. (The same is true for the bachelorette party.) For further tips on being a long-distance bridesmaid, see Handling Common Challenges (page 21).

THE BACHELORETTE PARTY (INCLUDING GIFT): $25–$150

Since the cost of bachelorette festivities is nearly always split equally among the bridesmaids, chances are your share won't be excessive. Remember that it's fine to ask everyone who comes to chip in, so if the guest list includes, say, the bride's friends from work, they should also contribute.

Smart Savings

* Save loads on games or invitations by using our free downloadable templates (www.chroniclebooks.com/bridesmaidguide).

* Host a fabulous house party, so the budget for booze and food is fixed.

* Feed the girls at home before you hit the town, so the entire group doesn't end up eating out at an expensive restaurant.

* Select a gift that everyone can agree on, purchase it in advance, and split the cost.

* Generally, the planning of this event is more democratic than that of the shower, so join the committee early and offer thoughtful budgetary cautions. As with the shower, though, the maid of honor often takes the lead.

* If you live far away and can't afford to fly out for the party, you may gracefully decline the invitation. For further tips on being a long-distance bridesmaid, see Handling Common Challenges (page 21).

BUDGET WORKSHEET

Bridesmaid responsibility	Estimate	Actual cost
The dress	$150–$600	$
Shoes and lingerie	$75–$250	$
Hair, makeup, and accessories	$50–$350	$
Transportation/lodging	$200–$1,000+	$
A wedding gift to the couple	$50–$200	$
The shower (including gift)	$50–$200	$
The bachelorette party (including gift)	$25–$150	$
TOTAL	**$600–$2,750**	$

SUMMARY

At the low end, you are looking at spending hundreds of dollars. Now breathe deeply and remember that you love this girl, and that what goes around comes around. If you try all the Smart Savings ideas and still feel totally strapped, it's time to have a heart-to-heart with the bride, or get creative and cut the costs of parties and gifts with some serious DIY. Keep coming back to the budget worksheet (page 41), and adjust the amounts as you receive information (use pencil). You can't always control how much you'll have to spend, but at least you'll know how deep you're diving into the hole!

Ten Signs the Bride Is Taking Her Bridal Blogs and Magazines Too Seriously

Even the most practical-minded bride can be reduced to mush by the pressure cooker of the wedding industry. Watch for these signs that she's starting to lose it, and take whatever steps are necessary to help her regain her wits.

She crosses every bakery in town off her list because none of them can get an exact color match between the bridesmaid gowns and the frosted doughnuts on the dessert table.

She reserves a reception table for her "Knotties" (her posting pals on The Knot Web site) even though she's never met them in person.

She insists that the bridesmaids hand-make crepe paper peonies, complete with biologically accurate stamens and petals, to wear in their hair on the day of the wedding.

She requests that each bridesmaid provide a professional head shot, an artfully written bio, and detailed measurements to be posted on the "Attendants" page of her wedding Web site.

She wants you and the other bridesmaids to create organza slipcovers tied with ribbons and festooned with fresh flowers for two hundred aluminum folding chairs.

On the morning of the wedding, she hands out craft punches to the bridal party and asks you to make snowflakes from silver paper—enough to fill a five-gallon bucket—to toss during her grand exit after the reception.

She requests that you and the other bridesmaids purchase expensive matching seamless bodysuits to wear beneath your sheath dresses, saying, "No panty lines at my wedding!"

She e-mails the bridesmaid team details about a protein-rich diet everyone should follow so their hair is stronger and shinier for the wedding.

In love with the trendy idea of cake jewelry, she wants to spend more on sparkling medallions of Swarovski crystals to adorn the wedding cake than on the groom's wedding ring.

She is Botoxing her armpits—which involves lots of needles and thousands of dollars—so she won't sweat in her dress.

Bridesmaid Calendar

The maid of honor (or a local bridesmaid, if the maid of honor lives in another state or is otherwise occupied), in addition to hosting and attending the pre-wedding parties, has the responsibility of attending a variety of pre-wedding appointments with the bride. Use this schedule to forecast when duty might call.

AN APPOINTMENTS CHECKLIST

✳ **Six Months to One Year before the Wedding**
Help the bride shop for her wedding dress (and for the bridesmaids' dresses, if she so desires). This may entail visiting numerous bridal boutiques, both nearby and out of town. Free up your weekends. This can be time-consuming work, but it has the potential to be high-quality girl time.

* **Two to Three Months before the Wedding**
  Attend the bride's dress fittings. Because you are her honor attendant, you should try to attend at least two. Ask the seamstress for tips on how to "bustle her train," if necessary. (These days, some gowns have trains attached with hooks and eyes or Velcro tape for easy removal.) You may also ask for tips on what product would best remove stains from the wedding dress fabric, so you can keep a bottle handy on the wedding day. Always deferring to the bride, and her mother if she attends the fitting, offer your observations of the alterations as they happen. If an altered bust or waistline doesn't look right to you, gently express your opinion. Watch the bride closely, and take your cues from her. If she looks as if she wants to say something, jump in there.

* **One Month to Six Weeks before the Wedding**
  Attend her trial hair and makeup appointments. You know what looks good on her—and what doesn't—and if that dark eye shadow makes her look like a drag queen, say so.

* **One to Two Days before the Wedding**
  Go for a manicure and pedicure with the bride. This is not a command performance, but an all-girl session at the salon is always a hoot. If you are the maid of honor, find out the timing for the bride's hair/makeup appointments and photo sessions on the wedding day. Any heads-up you can give the bridesmaid team about where the bride needs them to be is helpful at this point.

* **The Day of the Wedding**
  Accompany the bride to her hair and makeup appointments, unless she feels more comfortable going alone. Join her and all the maids for any planned group photo sessions (these are often scheduled a few hours in advance of the ceremony).

All about the Dress

A bride may consult her bridesmaids about the cost, color, and style of the bridesmaid dresses—but it is common, and perfectly acceptable, for her to choose and assign the dresses without consulting you.

SURVIVAL STRATEGIES

With the dress often begins the torture: the exorbitant Grecian-style emerald dress that makes you feel like the Jolly Green Giant and zeroes out your savings account; the strapless red velvet minidress that might be more welcome at Hooters; the frilly taffeta overstuffed-Barbie-doll number; the plain-Jane, high-waisted, six-year-old's recital dress. Sadly, fashion tragedies happen at weddings all the time—and you may very well be the victim of such misfortune. Still, wearing a bad outfit isn't the only thing that can go wrong when it comes to bridesmaid dresses. Follow this short list of tips and you should survive the dress experience with style.

PREPARE TO SHOP

If you will be shopping for and trying on bridesmaid dresses with a group, plan ahead and bring heels and appropriate undergarments (a good strapless bra you already own should do). Even a fabulous gown will look unbelievably bad if you're wearing a sports bra and sneakers. To ensure the gown truly fits well, remember to sit down and shimmy around while wearing it so you know movement doesn't cause problems.

DON'T SIZE DOWN

This might sound self-explanatory, but it has been the downfall of many a bridesmaid. Remember that dresses can always be taken in, but you can't make them bigger. Most bridesmaid dress designers offer their own size charts which you should consult carefully; to ensure proper fit, have your measurements taken by a professional seamstress or a friend (someone besides yourself) while wearing the undergarments you plan to wear with the dress. Don't size down because you plan to lose weight before the wedding or think squeezing into a too-small dress will help you avoid the cost of alterations. If your dress splits up the back when you bend over to fuss with your shoe on the wedding day, you'll pay a price that can't be measured in money.

CONFIRM YOUR ORDER

If the dress was an online order, open the box as soon as it arrives. It's not unheard of for a bridesmaid to receive something in a different style or color than what the bride supposedly ordered. Make sure you know the return policy before the purchase and build in enough time to exchange it should you receive the wrong dress or one with puckered fabric or a faulty zipper.

FIND A TAILOR

If you are unhappy with the fit of the dress, find a good seamstress. Tailoring can do wonders to make that shapeless gown conform to your curves. Find someone you can trust by asking around for recommendations or check WeddingWire (www.weddingwire.com), a resource for brides that includes user reviews of vendors organized by region, including those who specialize in wedding and bridesmaid dress alterations. Although perhaps not as trustworthy, online retailer reviews at a site such as Yelp (www.yelp.com) can also provide guidance. Wear the same undergarments to the fitting you'll wear on the wedding day since these can make a big difference in fit.

WHEN THE BRIDE LETS YOU CHOOSE

It's increasingly common for a bride to give her bridesmaids flexibility around their wedding day attire. Rather than assigning a specific dress that everyone must purchase, she provides some basic guidelines and leaves you in the driver's seat. Bonus! In any of the scenarios described below, you will have sartorial freedom—with which comes great responsibility.

SHE CHOOSES A CONVERTIBLE DRESS

Also called an infinity dress, this style can be twisted and tied into several different looks, including strapless, halter, one-shoulder, or deep V-neck. This is a huge plus because you can wear it in the most flattering style for you (just pay attention at that twist-and-tie tutorial!) while the bride gets to feel secure knowing bridesmaids will all be wearing the

same color and fabric. It can be a great addition to your wardrobe because it's simple and versatile and you can wear it again and again.

SHE CHOOSES THE STYLE AND COLOR

In this case, the bride supplies two simple style directives and lets you run with it them, instructing all maids to find a black cocktail dress, or something champagne and ankle-length. She may send a color swatch in the mail (or direct you to www.pantone.com) so you have something to match to.

SHE CHOOSES THE DESIGNER AND COLOR

The bride may select a designer and a color and ask each girl to choose her favorite dress accordingly. For example, she may send you to J. Crew online and ask you to select any bridesmaid style in peony pink. This option works in regular stores as well as online: You might be asked to visit a store like David's Bridal, which has locations nationwide, and select any bridesmaid dress in the store in her chosen color.

SHE CHOOSES COORDINATED SEPARATES

This is a great option because, with luck, you'll be able to wear the items again and again after the wedding. An example: The bride directs you to buy a top and a floor-length skirt in platinum, choosing your favorite style from several options. Separates can be on the pricier side, but if you can wear that platinum top time and again with black pants, it's a good return on your investment.

SHE CHOOSES NOT TO CHOOSE

Beware the bride who insists on saying "Buy whatever you want." In truth, most brides will have some idea of what your dress should look like and, at the very least, will know what they don't want you to wear. (Polka dots?) Once you have a few key details, conduct your dress search without her help. Likely, she gave you the responsibility so she could deal with other matters. A couple of pluses: One, you don't have to tell anyone where you found it—so consider going through a friend's closet! Two, you don't have to tell anyone how much you spent.

THE WORD ALERT: *PANTONE*

If you get a Pantone chip in the mail from the bride, don't fret. This is in fact a wedding tool—and you'll use it as a reference to select the color of your bridesmaid dress. Pantone is the world-renowned color authority that has provided graphic designers with a standard language for color for decades. Since their matching system enables great precision when it comes to sharing ideas about color, doesn't it make sense that brides would want in on the game? Recently, the Dessy Group, a major player in the bridesmaid dress business, partnered with Pantone to make these professional color-matching services available to brides via free color chips that can be requested on their Web site (www.dessy.com).
✳ **USAGE:** The bride says, *"The color is called quartz, but it's hard to describe—use the Pantone chip to match."*

FABULOUS TIP
HOW TO AVOID OFFENDING SOMEONE IMPORTANT
When wedding strife strikes and key players are acting kooky, the urge to unload your opinion can be irresistible—but weddings are not the time to tell the bride what you really think. Confide in a taxi driver or a friend who will not be attending the wedding. Do a full visual check of all compass points before getting into the gab, to rule out the possibility of being overheard by someone involved with the wedding.

TIPS FOR HAPPY TOES

As with the dress, you are responsible for buying the shoes to go with your ensemble. Some brides will stick with traditional dyed-to-match shoes, while others will opt for high-fashion footwear. For example, a bride who asked her bridesmaids to wear any black cocktail dress they want might choose a very specific shoe—say, a pink patent pump with a black bow—to create a coordinated look. Footwear is an increasingly popular way to personalize the attendants' attire. These days, whether it's crystal flip-flops at a beach wedding or cowboy boots for a rustic ceremony, anything goes. Follow these tips for happy toes, and whatever shoes you're wearing will feel like the perfect glass slipper.

✳ Remember to try on shoes in the late afternoon, when your feet can swell to half a size larger than they are in the morning. Stand in the shoes and take a quick walk around the store to make sure they don't slide off easily or rub uncomfortably.

✳ If you are going the dyed-pumps route, be aware that they can shrink when dyed. Going up a half size when you purchase the shoes could save you from being hobbled on the dance floor. Better too big than too small, since you can always wear foot liners inside the shoes for extra padding and a closer fit.

✳ Often, brides will give general guidelines for purchasing shoes, such as "black strappy sandals." When this is the case, feel free to bargain shop, but don't buy cheap, uncomfortable shoes just to save money. As a bridesmaid, you may be on your feet for eight hours straight.

✳ Wear them around the house in the week preceding the wedding. Breaking in shoes on the dance floor is never pleasant.

✳ Bring an extra pair. Satin ballet flats won't take up much room in a bag, and you can slip into them late-night if you just can't stand your shoes any longer.

The Better Bust Bra Chart

Bridesmaids who forgo bras deserve a round of applause for their daring, but for those who require some lift—either because the strapless dress demands it, or because you prefer support when performing for a crowd—here is the last word on what to buy for which dress.

STRAPLESS, ONE-SHOULDER, OR OFF-THE-SHOULDER DRESS

* **Bustier:** Encircles the torso while pushing up the bosom; if the dress has a low-cut back or you have a voluptuous figure, a bustier is preferable to the more flimsy strapless bra. Look for seamless styles that provide extra slimming since they provide coverage from the waist up.

* **Strapless bra:** Look for cups that lie flat against the ribs, and be sure the back doesn't ride up. If you will wear a one-shoulder dress and want extra support, a strapless with clear convertible straps might enable you to sneak one shoulder strap in.

* **Adhesive bra:** Two silicone cups designed to adhere to the body eliminate the need for straps. Follow the instructions closely, and a good-quality adhesive bra should stay put through a wedding and reception. To maximize cleavage, look for cups that attach with a front hook. These are a good choice for backless styles—not that we've seen too many backless bridesmaid gowns.

HALTER DRESS

* **Convertible or multiway bra:** The removable straps can be taken off and reattached to create numerous bra styles, including strapless, one strap, halter, classic, V-front, crossfront, or crossback.

DEEP V-NECK DRESS

✳ **Plunge bra:** A very deep U-shaped scoop allows you to get full support even with plunging necklines; for maximum versatility, look for a version that comes with straps that convert to halter, crossback, or classic.

SHEATH OR OTHER FORMFITTING DRESS

✳ **Seamless bodysuit:** Gives the smooth, sleek lines that this dress style demands. For more shaping and support, you can choose a stretch body dress that acts as both a slip and a bodysuit.

BETTER BUST ACCESSORIES

✳ **Double-sided tape:** Secure halters, bra straps, or wrap styles with this adhesive tape specifically made to gently adhere to skin and fabric.

✳ **Stay cups or gel petals:** You can find these gentle adhesive discs in versions designed to provide coverage only (read: prevent nipple show-through) and sturdier ones that give push-up support.

✳ **Replacement straps:** If you lost the straps to a convertible bra you already own, know that Victoria's Secret (www.victoriassecret.com) and other lingerie sites sell clear straps separately.

BETTER BUST MUSTS

✳ Try your undergarments on under your dress in approximately the same light in which you will be standing—sunlight if the wedding will be held outdoors, and so on. Have a friend (preferably an honest one) look for visible panty lines or bra or underwear lace appearing through the sheer dress material.

✳ Wear the undergarments out once, to make sure they don't chafe uncomfortably.

✳ Consider the potential weather. Will the ceremony be outside in the sun? No matter how much you like the idea of a seamless bodysuit, it won't be worth it if it makes you sweat like crazy. Go for a pair of simple body-shaping underwear instead—just remember to change out of those big beige underpants before you get some hot action.

Bridesmaids' Astrologer

Who's that bride? Prepare for your job as bridesmaid by looking at her stars.

✸ THE ARIES BRIDE
March 21–April 19
The energetic, laugh-a-minute Ram bride will be a blast to work for—she'll generally keep her sense of humor and make sure those pre-wedding parties rock until dawn. But, bridesmaids, be forewarned: Her spontaneous, fiery nature means that she may change her mind at the last second about things you thought were written in stone, like when you are scheduled to give your speech, or whether you'll have to dance with the best man. Rams are fashion-forward—she may ask you to wear something rather wild for the wedding. **Bridesmaid motto:** Be prepared for anything.

✸ THE TAURUS BRIDE
April 20–May 20
Put away your glitter eye shadow: This classy, earthy lady has a healthy respect for tradition, and her wedding will be about simple elegance. She insists on high quality in every department, from classy gowns to gourmet food and drink. (She would rather have salmon tartare at her bachelorette party than a male stripper.) Lucky for you, the Bull bride is one of the calmest in the zodiac, and you can count on her to pick you a fabulous dress—but be prepared to spend on stylish threads and sophisticated celebrations. **Bridesmaid motto:** Put on the ritz.

✸ THE GEMINI BRIDE
May 21–June 20
A bride born under this mercurial sign will rarely take the traditional, well-trodden route to the altar, and her ceremony will be as creative and interesting as the guests—a large crowd, since this sign attracts friends so effortlessly. As her bridesmaid, relieve her frequently with cocktails and encouragement since she'll be so busy dealing with the endless receiving line. Ruled by the Twins, the Gemini bride may be indecisive when planning the details; listen patiently to her myriad ideas, and help her choose one path from the thousands of possibilities she perceives. **Bridesmaid motto:** I am a rock.

✸ THE CANCER BRIDE
June 21–July 22
The Crab bride prefers to lead—not be led—and will have very specific ideas about wedding details. You would be wise to run the bridal party invitation lists by her and her mother, to whom she is close and whom she will want involved in planning details. Don't let her confident manner make you feel

unnecessary. In fact, she values your opinion highly. The slightest perceived criticism from a friend or mother-in-law will make the sensitive Cancerian retreat inside her shell. Encourage her to communicate her smallest concerns, and troubleshoot when others act insensitively. **Bridesmaid motto:** Don't worry; be happy.

✳ THE LEO BRIDE

July 23–August 22

Don't get angry when this bride has moments of arrogance or vanity—she can't avoid them any more than she can deny her party-loving nature. Besides, few brides appreciate loyalty and faithfulness in friends as much as the mighty Lion, and you'll feel the love when she thanks you and the other maids with loving tears, kisses, and public praise at the wedding. Be sure to plan a fabulous night out on the town with the ladies—with this bride at the helm, the bachelorette party will be an extraordinary evening. **Bridesmaid motto:** Keep your eyes on the bride.

✳ THE VIRGO BRIDE

August 23–September 22

This perfectionist bride will tirelessly devote herself to planning the wedding, and you'd better be prompt at all the fittings, appointments, and pre-wedding events. Under stress, she may snap at you—but if you're an old friend, you know her bark is worse than her bite. What she really needs from you more than elaborate party planning is compassion and emotional support, despite her rather self-sufficient appearance. This bride can take care of the details, and your job is to provide the love—and loosening up—she needs in order to feel grounded and happy. **Bridesmaid motto:** Be there with bells on.

✳ THE LIBRA BRIDE

September 23–October 22

Don't wait around for indecisive Libra, the sign of the Balanced Scales, to give you a color scheme or a to-do list. The fewer planning questions you ask her, the better. This classy lady will pull off an elegant wedding, but even she may not know how it happened. Spend your time planning a bridal shower or bachelorette party that will please her picky palate—but before you break a sweat about breaking the bank, keep in mind that well-mannered Libra would be mortified if she thought you were spending more than you could afford. **Bridesmaid motto:** Don't ask; don't tell.

✸ THE SCORPIO BRIDE

October 23–November 21

Her wedding means more than most people's—at least that's how this intense bride perceives things. This bride can be a privacy freak, so you will be required to keep her secrets about the groom's dark side or her wild past, or keep quiet about family flaps at the wedding. At some point she may lose her tight emotional control and get wildly jealous about the groom's bachelor party or enraged at the careless caterers. Soothe her with her favorite sedative—a show of your love and loyalty. When the wedding day comes and this emotionally deep lady says her vows, there won't be a dry eye in the house. **Bridesmaid motto:** Fasten your seat belt.

✸ THE SAGITTARIUS BRIDE

November 22–December 21

She can be a little bossy, but will you ever have fun! From dress fittings to parties to the ceremony itself, the Archer bride will almost never lose her buoyant enthusiasm. Only when this extremely independent woman clashes with others over wedding plans will she get upset (weddings

offer the frank Sagittarian lady many opportunities to stick her foot in her mouth). The two of you might even squabble—but this girl never holds a grudge, and if you can forgive her in the same generous spirit, the wedding will be a laugh riot from start to finish. **Bridesmaid motto:** Roll with the punches.

THE CAPRICORN BRIDE
December 22–January 19
Your job—and it's a tough one—is to help this ambitious, industrious bride put aside her perfectionist tendencies and have some fun! Surprise parties are a good idea, since she can't fret over them or try to do all the hard work herself. A Capricorn will rarely ask for what she needs—affection and indulgence—so plan lots of fabulous events, especially ones that distract her from fussy wedding details, and appeal to her great sense of humor. Family is very important to her, so make sure they approve of you; help them have fun at wedding events, or she might get tense. **Bridesmaid motto:** Forget perfection—let's party.

THE AQUARIUS BRIDE
January 20–February 18
The Water Bearer bride has loads of friends—too many, you might think once you start trying to plan her bridal parties. Wildly gregarious,

she tends to bond with people of every race, age, and gender, and she embraces their diverse sexual, religious, and political preferences. She doesn't want anyone to feel left out. Carry a cell phone to coordinate parties and be prepared to smooth over any social gaps that may crop up between her far-flung friends when they get together. **Bridesmaid motto:** The more, the merrier.

THE PISCES BRIDE
February 19–March 20
This idealistic bride may be moody in the months before the wedding, feeling that the sacredness of love is being trampled by the wedding's endless, practical details. In fact, maybe she would have eloped, except that her romantic streak can't resist a wedding shared with family and friends. This sign is ruled by Neptune, the planet of illusion and fantasy—the very things that make weddings magical. She may search tirelessly for the perfect gown, but don't mistake this trait for materialism. In her heart, all she really cares about is that the emotional vibrations are right— among her friends, at the pre-wedding parties, and on the day itself. **Bridesmaid motto:** Feel the love.

3

THE BRIDAL SHOWER

Golden Rules

For most of us, planning the bridal shower is hands-down the most daunting part of being a bridesmaid or maid of honor. (If everything goes according to plan, this party will only happen once in her lifetime!) This section includes everything you need to succeed: scores of creative shower themes, fun group games, and easy party favors, plus the essential etiquette for every occasion. But using these party-planning tips is only half of the equation. The real secret behind any fabulous bridal party is attitude. Let these golden rules be your trusted guide.

PERSONALIZE THE PARTY

Not every bridal shower needs a menu of finger sandwiches and tea, nor does opening gifts have to be the main attraction. Why? Because every bride is different. The thing to remember is that you know her—even if she was a childhood friend you've lost touch with more recently—so use that knowledge to your advantage. As a first step, dream up some unique shower themes that celebrate her personality and her history with the groom. Would she love a "Sweets and Snowballs" theme because he proposed on a ski trip—or would she find that cloying? A creative team of fabulous bridesmaids will find a way to personalize each party in a way that makes the bride proud.

NEVER ASSUME ANYTHING ABOUT INVITATION LISTS

Even though the bride has confided that she can't stand her fiancé's bossy sister—and you happen to dislike the woman, too—this doesn't mean you can leave her out of the bridal party loop. Weddings are not about whom you like, and they often aren't even about whom the bride likes. They're about family. Consult with the bride and use discretion. (Read: Don't post details online about when or where a party will be, for example, if there's a chance that others who are not invited might see them and feel excluded.)

PLAY GAMES (EVEN IF YOU DON'T WANT TO)

If a rousing game of Toilet Paper Bride isn't your cup of tea, play something else—but for goodness' sake, don't skip the games completely. Bridal showers often bring together people of disparate ages and backgrounds; games are truly the best way to break the ice. Once folks stop feeling self-conscious and engage with each other, the fun can begin. Check out our Great Games (page 78), and pick something that will appeal to the bulk of the crowd.

REMEMBER YOUR PECKING ORDER

The maid of honor is in charge. Although she and the bridesmaids work as a team, the primary honor attendant should have the final say in any contentious decision. If she lives out of town and can only fly in for the wedding, a local bridesmaid might step in and fill her role during the pre-wedding festivities. It is helpful to have someone in charge of the troupe with so many decisions to be made, so whoever takes the wheel, respect her authority.

Bridal Shower Q&A

Bridal showers are generally held two months to two weeks before the wedding. They can be small, intimate, and ladies-only, or they can be big affairs that include the groom and his friends and family—but the main point is to honor the bride and "shower" her with gifts. If this is your first tour of duty as a bridesmaid, our Q&A below should answer all your basic questions, so you can move forward to plan your fabulous event.

Who Hosts? Hosting can be undertaken by the maid of honor, the bridal party, or a female relative or friend of the bride's. Traditionally, the maid of honor kicks off the planning, but if she lives far away or is otherwise unavailable, any bridesmaid can step in. In today's world of long-distance friendships, hosting a bridal shower is defined less by your role in the bride's wedding than by your proximity to the bride and her family and your willingness to play hostess. If you throw a shower, it may not be the only one. Although it was previously viewed as poor etiquette for the bride's mother to host a shower (too obvious a bid for booty), today it's common and considered acceptable. Coworkers may step in to throw an additional event. With so many parties potentially happening, check with the bride (and to be safe, her mother) to make sure that the date you choose isn't double-booked. Use Doodle (see page 20) to get the ball rolling.

Who Pays? The hostess underwrites the party. If the maid of honor hosts, it is perfectly acceptable for her to ask the bridesmaids if they are willing to split some or all of the cost (as long as what she's planning is budget-friendly). While talking about money during celebratory times can make you feel like Ebenezer Scrooge, being tactful and clear early on will prevent problems later. Keep track of who contributed what, and solicit funds when necessary. Do not, however, discuss budgetary issues with the bride. Another don't: asking the bride's relatives to chip in financially for the shower or bachelorette. Feel free to accept any gracious offers, but do not ask for contributions outright.

Who's Invited? Bridesmaids, members of both families, and close friends may be invited. The gathering might be just ladies or, in the case of a Jack-and-Jill shower, include both genders. Everyone invited to the shower should be invited to the wedding, although there are exceptions—for example, when the shower is thrown by coworkers, or when the couple is having a very small wedding at a faraway location. Some guests will be invited to one shower only, and others, especially the maid of honor and bridesmaids, may be invited to several. (You need bring a gift only to the first one, although you may bring a token like chocolates or fresh flowers to subsequent events.)

A SHOWER IN TEN SIMPLE STEPS

1. Get the bridesmaids on board.
2. Choose a theme.
3. Select a venue.
4. Make the guest list.
5. Send the invitations.
6. Create a menu.
7. Find the favors.
8. Select the games.
9. Buy your gift.
10. Have fun!

Choosing a Theme

A shower theme can be traditional, like high tea, or alternative, like a "Go Green" eco party. Whether you are hosting alone or with a whole team of bridesmaids, and whether the shower is for eight people or eighty, choosing a theme will make the shower planning easier.

Enlist your bridesmaids (use e-mail if the group is far-flung) for help with brainstorming. As you consider what she might like, also keep in mind your budget, the general size of the guest list, the possible venues, and the type of crowd you'll be catering to. Once you settle on a theme, you can translate the idea into coordinating menus, unique favors, and décor that will delight the bride and all the guests. This section includes All-Purpose Shower Themes (which provide general ideas to spark inspiration) and Total Package Shower Themes (which provide detailed ideas for favors, gifts, and games that weave the theme into every thoughtful detail). In short, here is everything you need to turn a simple shower into a superlative celebration.

 ## ALL-PURPOSE SHOWER THEMES

Find inspiration in one of these five basic themes that will give immediate structure to your shower planning. Each one can easily be tailored to suit the bride's special interests.

HIRE A PRO

Whether it's cooking, cocktail making, or Shiatsu massage, it's popular to turn the shower into a (fun) teachable moment. Hiring a pro to teach the bride—and her lucky guests—a thing or two gives the event structure and take-away value. These showers tend to be nontraditional and may be scheduled in the evening, so only consider this option if it seems appropriate for the guest list. Opt for personalized favors in sync with the theme. If it's a cocktail class, order coasters imprinted with the wedding date or the couple's initials and wrap them in ribbon-tied pairs for the guests to take home.

GET CRAFTY

The idea here is to ask guests to customize something special for the bride as part of the event. Something as simple as a scrapbooking shower, where each guest brings treasured photos of her with the bride, and the host supplies a scrapbook station with specialty scissors, stickers, and other adornments, can result in a great keepsake. All the host is then responsible for is putting each guest's page into a special book for the bride. Another option is to host the event at a local pottery studio where guests can create hand-painted gifts for the bride. Or keep it edible with an adorable cupcake bar. Offer plain vanilla and chocolate cupcakes in festive gold foil wrappers and set up a buffet of colorful toppings—pastel icings, bright candies, slivered almonds, cookie pieces, toasted coconut— so each person can decorate her own. Have the bride choose her favorite for dessert and whoever made that cupcake wins a prize.

CHOOSE A DESTINATION

From afternoon tea at a fancy hotel to an upscale country club luncheon, hosting bridal showers outside the home is nothing new. In this day and age, all kinds of venues work, from spas and cupcake boutiques to beauty bars and cocktail lounges. Any fun destination is fair game, as long as it's appropriate for the bride and her guests. And these days, many a bridesmaid team, when they can afford it, choose to host the shower at a fancy hotel suite rather than someone's tiny living room. But this is just the tip of the iceberg. Like bachelorette parties, showers can be destination events, too, taking place over a weekend at the beach, a country house, or even (expensively) Vegas or Miami. If this is the case, take the destination bachelorette party off your dance card—you're not made of money, after all.

GIVE BACK

Whether it's being good to the Earth by going green or asking guests to give to charity in lieu of gifts, brides who love to give back are making their voices heard. Host a sophisticated eco-themed shower with professionally designed e-mail invites (classy but still paper saving), organic food and décor, and a request for green gifts like bamboo sheets or artwork from recycled materials. If it's a charity shower, have the bride select a few favorite causes so guests may donate in her name. Rather than making opening gifts the main event, participate in a neighborhood tree planting or find other ways to put the guests' energies toward doing good.

CELEBRATE HER HOBBY

Does she love hiking, beachcombing, or mountain biking? Host an outdoor adventure shower. Ask guests to bring gifts on the theme and offer goody bags with sunscreen, lip balm, and keepsake water bottles. This is perfect for an active and unconventional bunch of guests who are game to join in the bride's preferred activity. If she loves to dig in the dirt, host a garden shower. Ask guests to keep gifts to garden tools and accessories, and round out the event with a menu of locally grown food, outdoor-inspired décor, and easy favors like seed packets and small decorative planters.

❗ THE WORD ALERT: *SURPRISE!*

Surprise showers are fun, but be sensitive to the bride who doesn't like being caught off guard. Give the bride a reason to dress up if you do plan one (use lunch at a fancy restaurant as your red herring event) so she'll look cute in the pictures. When in doubt, opt out. Involving the bride can make the planning much easier and the shower more fun.

✳ **USAGE:** A bridesmaid says to the bride, *"I've been so good about keeping your shower a surprise! Whoops."*

TOTAL PACKAGE SHOWER THEMES

Details make a difference. That's why our descriptions below offer the total entertaining package, with specific ideas for décor, favors, gifts, and games that will coordinate with your theme.

"WEAR YOUR WHITES" SHOWER

Easy Concept: For the sporting bride-to-be, what could be more fun than an afternoon of croquet or badminton—especially when the real point is to drink mint juleps and wear crisp whites? This shower is great for warm-weather months and large groups. While an outdoor location is necessary, athletic skills are optional!

Hostess Hotline: Find a fun location outdoors—any grassy backyard or pleasant park will do. (If you have trouble finding a spot, persevere and make some inquiries; perhaps the bride's aunt has a lovely home that would be the perfect venue.) Plan a buffet menu of cool drinks and elegant picnic fare. On the day of the party, arrive early to set up the croquet or badminton set, and learn the rules if you don't already know them. Once guests arrive, ply them with food and cocktails while clearly explaining how to play. Let the games begin, and you've got a party.

Gifts and Favors: Anything white. Gifts can be as practical as crisp white sheets, white table linens, or white kitchen appliances, or more conceptual, like a framed black-and-white photograph or a fabulous bottle of white wine. For favors, affix stickers printed with the couple's wedding date to clear ribbon-tied bags filled with white saltwater taffy or white Jordan almonds (download sticker templates at www .chroniclebooks.com/bridesmaid.guide).

Great Game: Play a theme-party version of *The Newlywed Game.* In advance, ask the groom questions that involve the color white. For vacation, would he rather go white-water rafting or snowboard on fresh powder? Which item of white clothing does he wear most often: white BVDs, white socks, or tight white T-shirts? Would he rather listen to the White Stripes (indie rock), Whitesnake ('80s metal), Average White Band (disco), or Barry White (soul)? The bride—and all the guests—have to pick which answers they think the groom would choose. The more ridiculous the questions, the better. (If you don't have time to get his answers in advance, use the bride's answers as the key.) The guest who guesses the most answers correctly wins a prize.

DINNER PARTY SHOWER

Easy Concept: A dinner party will always be a hit with a food-loving bride and her pals. The event can be simple and potluck-style, or you can give it a surprising twist by hosting a reality chef show–inspired competition. Just be sure the guest list is no more than about a dozen, and that all the guests are comfortable in the kitchen.

Hostess Hotline: Is she a Francophile? Ask guests to bring their favorite Gallic dish, play Edith Piaf, and pour Côtes du Rhône. Or, go for something more daring: If you have access to a reasonably sized kitchen, surprise the bride with a little competitive cooking. Invite guests to rounds of a ten-minute competition where, with the timer going, participants have to make an appetizer from the ingredients laid out in the kitchen. (Keep the participants to three or four people at once.) Label the ingredients well, providing several bowls of each type so everyone has easy access. Make your choices a little wacky but with the potential to taste good in combination. Think potato chips, cream cheese, and sun-dried tomatoes, or sourdough bread, asparagus, and cheddar cheese. With everyone running around, good times are sure to ensue. At the bell, the bride tastes to select her favorite, and the winner gets a prize. Of course, you'll want to have plenty of regular appetizers and main-course foods on hand since these competitive appetizers might not be so edible.

Gifts and Favors: Specialty cookware, cookbooks, gourmet foods, and other kitchen-related items make great gifts. Or have the whole group pitch in for a year-long subscription to a monthly food club—at online gourmet purveyors like Zingerman's (www.zingermans.com), you'll find choices ranging from rare olive oils and specialty cheeses to brownies and coffee beans. For favors, offer ribbon-tied bottles of balsamic vinegar or gourmet sea salt.

Games: Wrap a variety of spices—preferably those used in the dishes you're serving—in small aluminum packets with holes poked in them. Pass the packets around the circle so guests can sniff the packets and try to name each spice correctly. It's surprisingly hard! Similarly, you can play the game with wine in unmarked glasses or foil-wrapped gourmet cheese, with each blindfolded participant tasting the wine and cheese and making her guess. The one who has identified the most spices or other items correctly at the end of the round wins a prize.

THE WORD ALERT: *CANAPÉS*

If you know exactly what this word means, you probably own lots of cookbooks. If you don't know, here's a simple description: any type of delightful little snack served on tiny toast. Basic pronunciation: kah-nah-pay (and the last syllable sounds like the *é* in *café*). ✤ **USAGE:** The bride's mother says to you, ***"Are you planning on making canapés for the bridal shower?"*** Correct answer: ***"I'm still planning the menu."*** (Read: I'm the hostess, and I'll do what I please.)

COUPLES BARBECUE BASH

Easy Concept: Perfect for the easygoing bride who loves big, zany parties, this theme shower is great for including the guys. A large backyard or park lawn is ideal, so you can barbecue safely and have plenty of space to spread out during the games.

Hostess Hotline: Jack-and-Jill showers are most successful when they include themes that interest both the bride and groom. While many still feature the traditional gift-opening event, the main activities should be eating, drinking, and games—and when the guest list is large, you may dispense with opening the gifts altogether. (The bride and groom may feel relieved to get out of performing for such a large audience.) When it comes to being the hostess, the duties here are light! All you have to do is get some juicy steaks or burgers to throw on the grill, pick up a selection of salads and condiments at your local deli, and order a keg of cold beer. Although mixed showers are increasingly popular, be sure that the bride, and her mother, are on board for inviting the guys before you start the planning process.

Gifts: Barbecue-related items such as tongs, serving dishes, aprons, or cookbooks will work well; you can also expand the gift theme to include backyard items, from hammocks or casual lawn chairs to garden tools and plants. If the guest list is particularly large, however, you may want to omit gift suggestions and let people bring items from the registry, or whatever they think the couple will enjoy, ensuring that the bride and groom don't receive more outdoor accessories than would be useful.

Games: Split the crowd into teams, and pit the men against the women in a good-natured battle of the sexes. Kick off the competition by having the two teams compete to create the best burger combination, to be judged by the father of the bride. Or opt for traditional relays and games: Go for favorites like an egg-in-a-spoon relay (each team's player takes it to a designated spot and back without dropping it, then gives the egg and spoon to the next person in line) or a three-legged race (where you tie together pairs of people at the ankle, and the first couple to cross the finish wins). If you don't have enough space to play outdoors, you could have both teams compete to see who can build the larger structure out of playing cards.

BRIDAL TEA

Easy Concept: When the guest list includes ladies ages eight to eighty, a traditional tea party is an excellent way to entertain. Swap complicated shower themes and rowdy party games for a simple afternoon of charming conversation, delicious finger sandwiches, and strong tea served in delicate china cups.

Hostess Hotline: A pleasant, summery garden full of golden afternoon light is the ideal setting for this classic bridal event. Hire or borrow enough folding chairs or garden furniture so that the majority of folks can sit down, and consider making a special seat for the bride festooned with streamers, flowers, or white tulle, so she can sit in high style while opening her gifts. The buffet table should be a party highlight, with fresh flowers and a delicious array of treats. Lay out silver trays of finger sandwiches and plates of delicate lemon shortbread, fresh strawberries, currant scones, and clotted cream. Have tea cozies on hand to keep the teapots warm, and serve the tea with cream and sugar, or lemon, in delicate teacups with saucers. You may also serve a light cocktail, such as mimosas, or a chilled, crisp white wine.

Gifts: The traditional style of the party will inspire most guests to bring a traditional gift, either an item from the bridal registry or a gift for the couple's home. Spread the information about where the bride is registered by word of mouth or direct guests to the wedding Web site. If guests ask you for further guidance, tell them that any traditional item for the kitchen, bedroom, or bath would be welcomed.

Games: This classic tea party calls for the tried-and-true games that have become bridal shower standards. For ideas, see our section on Great Games (page 78).

If you prefer not to follow a theme, try simple entertaining options such as an evening of desserts and coffee or a casual midmorning brunch. Wish you'd reserved a special venue but didn't think to in advance? Think creatively—a cute bakery, art gallery, local coffee shop, or scenic park might be the perfect place to host your last-minute event. Since guests will bring gifts of their own choosing, you may choose to circulate, by word of mouth, the names of the places she's registered.

Selecting a Venue

Once a theme is selected—and approved by those who will cohost— you'll need to choose a venue before you can send out the invitations. Discuss the options in detail with the other bridesmaids helping to finance or host the event, and make sure they are all on board for the direction you take. If you will be renting a space or heading to a restaurant, get answers to key questions such as cost, cancellation policy, options for serving alcohol and playing music, and whether DIY decorating is an option. If it's at someone's home, find out how much seating is available—will everyone be comfortable and feel included? Additionally, plan how you'll set a festive mood in the space with details like soundtrack, lighting, and a pretty gift table.

Shower Invitations

Once you've consulted the bride about the guest list, you can dive into the invitations. Especially for a larger event, sending a save-the-date by e-mail or regular mail about six weeks prior is a good idea. (Long-distance friends or relatives looking into airfare will need at least this much warning.) One of the trickiest parts of the invitations is deciding how to handle informing guests about the bride's registry. Traditionally, this was only done by word of mouth. In today's world of looser etiquette, it's increasingly common to list the registry stores at the bottom of the invitation or include the bride's registry cards in the envelope. Keep in mind that this may be off-putting for guests with a keen sense of what's proper. Fortunately, the problem is solved if the bride has a wedding Web site; use technology to your advantage and simply direct folks to the URL (just make sure the bride's registry will be posted by the time invitations are received).

As for actual invitations, try to get those out about a month in advance. Paper invitations are most appropriate for a bridal shower. If you feel compelled to send them electronically, either by direct e-mail or via a service like Evite (www.evite.com), do so only for a small, casual affair that doesn't include the older generation. Consider that the majority of brides still expect paper invitations, and their prettiness and formality set the stage for the party. When you are ready to send them out, choose from one of these options:

✳ Download one of our *Bridesmaid Guide* shower invitation templates at www.chroniclebooks.com/bridesmaidguide; fill in the date, the time, and other details; and print on your home printer.

✳ Buy preprinted invitations and fill them out by hand.

✳ Hand-make cards. Use your home computer to print the invitation on sturdy card stock, then cover the card with sheer vellum attached by colorful ribbon threaded through a couple of punched holes.

✳ Find charming letterpress stationery that ties into the theme or speaks to the bride's passions. If he proposed at the beach, for example, find cards with a shell or starfish print. (Note: this option will cost more.)

✳ If you plan to write the invitations, you may word as follows:

You are invited to attend a shower
in honor of Sarah Putman
Sunday, May tenth, at five o'clock
3322 Santa Clara Street
San Francisco, California
Please RSVP to Emily Miller
by April 15
(415) 555-8605 or emily@gmail.com

Note: *If you wish to include the name of the host, the first line would read, "Emily Miller invites you to attend a shower in honor of…"*

If the event has a theme, such as a linen shower, you may insert that on the second line, above the date and time. Request RSVPs at least two weeks in advance of the event and choose one bridesmaid to be the point person, or, for large events, use an online RSVP service to keep track. Remember that ultimately, the wording of an invitation should clarify all the pertinent details. Along with basics like date and time, include defining factors like whether it's a surprise or if it's a coed event. Depending on the theme or venue, you could specify attire as cocktail, casual, or sporty. Run the guest list by the bride one last time before putting the envelopes in the mail—and remember that, despite the work involved, a carefully chosen or created invitation will always charm its recipients.

Shower Favors, Décor, and Details

• *Favors:* At an elegant gathering, offerings might include small potted plants, miniature books of poetry, soy candles or beeswax soaps, half bottles of champagne or chardonnay, gourmet jams or scone mixes, packets of seeds, or gift cards and stationery. For a crowd of ladies who appreciate kitsch, Magic 8 Balls, body glitter, astrology scrolls, nail polish, and mood rings make a fun mix of gifts. If you plan to give game prizes, be sure to have plenty on hand—for five group games, have around a dozen wrapped items. That way, if several people tie for first place, each can claim an award. If you will be simply giving the favors at the door, have enough for everyone, plus a few extras. Skip complicated handcrafted items, and don't break the bank on gifts for the guests. This party is more about the lovely bride than anyone else.

• *Décor:* Stick with easy decorations inspired by the theme—at a garden shower, for example, potted herbs in pretty planters might double as décor and favors for guests. Especially if you're hosting in a hotel suite or another location that's not homey, you'll need decorations to warm up the space. Go for floral arrangements that won't cost a mint but will have impact, like flowering branches in tall vases or bunches of bright Gerbera daisies. When shopping for extras like balloons, streamers, linens, and cocktail napkins, a fresh two-tone color palette will pull the look together; think tropical orange and hot pink, preppy green and white, or sophisticated metallics like silver and gold. Even something as simple as festoons of white tulle will remind guests of the impending wedding and make a memorable statement. Also, displaying a beautiful framed photograph of the bride and groom together is a nice touch.

• *Music:* Have quiet but mood-setting music on as guests arrive. When the games begin, you can turn down the volume, but from strains of classical Bach to mellow bossa nova, a soundtrack will help people relax upon arrival. It can also tie nicely into your shower theme.

• *Photos:* Appoint a bridal shower shutterbug. Her skill at taking digital photos isn't as important as her willingness to put aside her drink and focus on capturing the best, funniest, and most memorable moments of the shower. (Hint: Don't try to play photographer if you'll be busy with hosting duties.)

 ## SHOWER GIFT DOS AND DON'TS

At most bridal showers, the main event is watching the bride open her gifts. If the bride wants to avoid this display, consider a charity shower, where gifts won't be a feature (arrange a pretty, beribboned collection basket for donations to her choice of charity, with extra envelopes placed nearby for guests who forgot to bring one.) Otherwise, follow these Dos and Don'ts to keep the whole gift thing glitch-free.

• *Do plan ahead to make the gift-opening session quick and efficient.* Give various tasks to designated bridesmaids such as delivering gifts to the bride, dealing with discarded wrapping, recording the bride's reactions for a traditional shower game (see Wedding Night Preview, page 83); and making a list of who gave what so the bride can easily write thank-you notes later.

• **Don't spend too much.** Plan to spend somewhere between $25 and $50. According to etiquette, giving lavish presents at bridal showers is not in good taste. You don't want your shower to come off as a consumer frenzy where friends feel pressured to prove their buying power. The most appropriate and classic shower gift is a practical and affordable household item. So spread the news—and don't feel self-conscious if your gift seems simple in comparison to the others. As long as your offering is lovingly chosen and personally or prettily wrapped, it will be a welcome addition.

• **Do give one main gift.** If you are invited to attend more than one shower, you don't have to bring a gift to each event. Purchasing one gift that's substantial or meaningful is preferable to bringing smaller, cheaper gifts to each of the parties. Any thoughtful bride will understand that you simply can't afford to bring equally elegant gifts to all the showers. Similarly, graciously declining a second or third shower invitation is perfectly fine. After all, attending showers is just one of your duties, and surviving the long haul to the wedding without feeling harried is key to maintaining your fabulousness.

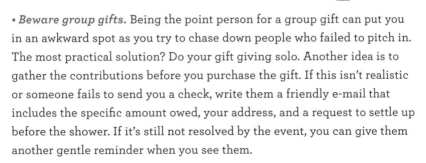

• **Beware group gifts.** Being the point person for a group gift can put you in an awkward spot as you try to chase down people who failed to pitch in. The most practical solution? Do your gift giving solo. Another idea is to gather the contributions before you purchase the gift. If this isn't realistic or someone fails to send you a check, write them a friendly e-mail that includes the specific amount owed, your address, and a request to settle up before the shower. If it's still not resolved by the event, you can give them another gentle reminder when you see them.

Gift Suggestions

Many showers have themes that provide guidelines for giving gifts. If there is no theme, check the bridal registry for gift ideas in your price range, let imagination be your guide, or consider some of the following ideas.

GREAT GIFTS

* Adorable retro apron and ribbon-tied spatulas

* Upscale "vows" box for wedding day keepsakes

* Clever his-and-hers key racks

* Decorative boxed wooden matches and bright votive holders from Etsy (www.etsy.com)

* Tiered porcelain server or colorful cake stand

* Themed cocktail gift, like margarita glasses plus fancy tequila

* Luxe eco-friendly bamboo towels or bed linens

* High-design magazine basket and a new subscription she'd love

* Monogrammed set of bright, casual napkins and serving tray

* A gift certificate to her favorite spa or restaurant

* Colorful Deruta-style serving bowls, plates, or pitchers

* For the gardener, hand-selected seed packets, garden tools, and accessories

* A cookbook and accessories on a theme—for example, a book on classic Spanish paella, paired with a pan and imported rice used in the traditional preparation of the dish

PERSONALIZED GIFTS

BRIDAL SHOWER SCRAPBOOK

No matter what type of bridal shower you host, making a scrapbook to commemorate the occasion is an extra special touch to make the event even more memorable for the bride.

Step One: Put one photo-savvy guest or bridesmaid in charge of snapping some fun, casual digital photos.

Step Two: Use a Web site like Shutterfly.com to order some prints for a scrapbook, or create a digital photo book (the more expensive option).

Step Three: If you opt for prints, buy a photo book—and make it fun! If she loves kitsch, score a puffy, glittery book from a kid's novelty shop and glue in the pictures; or go classic with black-and-white prints laid out in an tasteful photo album.

Step Four: Personalize the scrapbook by writing sweet and sassy notes in the margins (the most important part). Rely on the bridesmaids to provide editorial input after the party is over, or attempt to have the guests write personal notes in the scrapbook page margins while the bridal shower is underway. (Set up a writing station with the book and fun glitter pens in a quiet room so people can write unseen by the bride. Or provide cards for guests to write on, which you will place in the book later.)

Step Five: Add shower mementos like monogrammed napkins, lovely bits of ribbon, or scorecards from the games you played.

Optional Extras: If you're ambitious and good with follow-through, start the scrapbook at the bridal shower, but expand the idea to create a visual journal of her entire tour as a bride. Choose a durable, leather-bound book that will last forever, and include mementos from the bridal shower, the bachelorette party, the rehearsal dinner, and the wedding; invitations, photographs, copies of toasts and speeches, and notes from the bride's dearest friends and family members are welcome additions. Since creating such a scrapbook takes considerable time, money, and effort, you may consider giving it as the wedding gift—after all, memories are the best present of all. She'll be touched by your thoughtfulness every time she opens the book.

FABULOUS TIP ⫸⫸⫸➤

HOW TO DEAL WITH BIG SPENDERS

Some bridesmaids are constantly brainstorming new ideas for group shower gifts for the bride, even after the group has decided on one or two specific items. When this spendy bridesmaid pressures everyone else to make endless additional contributions, major friction and financial distress can ensue. Often, what makes this high-rolling girl so eager to empty her pockets (and yours) is guilt. Plagued with remorse about missing one of the bridal parties or an old friendship trauma—and hoping to redeem herself by giving presents—she pressures herself and everyone else into buying "just one more thing." When you are forced to deal with this big spender, politely explain that despite your never-ending love for the bride, you simply don't have any money left after buying the bridesmaid dress, arranging to attend the showers, and purchasing the gifts. As an alternative, you could offer to go in on the suggested gift as a wedding present instead of a shower gift.

A Shower Planning Checklist

Get on the ball early with this detailed to-do list.

✳ **Four Months before the Shower**
The truth is, although you can start planning four months in advance, you don't absolutely have to (call it honest procrastination). If you are eager to start planning, begin on the tasks listed below. Otherwise, just start mulling over some of the big things, like where you might hold the party and what style of entertaining your budget can accommodate.

✳ **Three Months Before the Shower**
Consult the bride, and decide on the guest list together. (If you're hosting a surprise shower, consult the bride's mother or another family member.)

Narrow down dates and contact key guests to see what days work. This may include the bride's mother, sisters, and aunts; her oldest friend from grade school who was invited to the wedding but can't make it; and the bridesmaids, of course.

Finalize the date and time of day.

Choose the location. If necessary, reserve the place and put down a deposit. If party rentals or caterers will be involved, book them.

Get the addresses, e-mails, and telephone numbers of everyone on the guest list.

✳ Two Months Before the Shower
Decide on a shower theme and location. Earlier is better, because it will establish the invitation style and type of food, drink, and atmosphere you want for the party.

Send out save-the-dates.

Finalize your choice of invitations and shop for them.

✳ One Month Before the Shower
Distribute invitations by mail. Only opt for e-mail invites if it's an eco-themed party (e.g., paperless) or the occasion is extremely casual.

Decide on games. They're the heart and soul of every fabulous shower.

Write a party to-do list. Enlist help from the bridesmaids by giving them specific tasks. For example, "Betty, could you watch the wine on the buffet table during the party, and bring out new chilled bottles when necessary?"

Make or purchase favors.

Buy your gift.

✳ The Week Before the Shower
Confirm RSVPs. (Have a point person chase down any replies that haven't come in.)

Call bridesmaids slated to bring key contributions such as food for the party, serving trays, music, or decorations to confirm.

Confirm food, flower, or cake orders, as well as delivery or pickup times.

Buy nonperishable groceries and liquor or wine.

Decide on decorations, estimate how long it will take you to put them up, and purchase necessary items.

Assemble and wrap favors.

Assemble everything you need for the shower games.

Decide what you'll wear. Seriously. Don't wait until the last minute and discover you forgot to dry-clean your cutest dress.

✳ The Day Before the Shower
Shop for perishables and prepare any food items that can be made in advance.

Get in touch with the bridesmaids to make sure they know their duties.

Run last-minute errands.

✳ The Day Of the Shower
Get to the party site early to set up decorations and seating.

Finish preparing food, or receive or pick up food orders.

Arrange flowers and food on tables.

Be fabulous!

Great Games

Looking for the perfect game to bring shower guests together without boring them to tears? Of course you are—every great bridesmaid is—and it can be quite a challenge, especially at a shower where the bride's prim aunts and sweet grandmother will be sitting right next to the bride's most outrageous, party-loving friends. The multipurpose, multigenerational games in these pages are the perfect solution, at once inexpensive to plan and easy to play. Many of them can be individually tailored and do double duty: Not only will they break the ice and get everyone laughing, they will also celebrate the bride's likes, her dislikes, her past, her present, and her future with the groom as splendidly as could any carefully crafted speech. And what could be more thoughtful than that?

One warning: Before you pick your game, imagine how it will strike your guests. If it focuses on the bride's childhood, newer acquaintances may feel left out. An overly libidinous game may offend the older folks. The best way to avoid ruffling feathers is to choose a funny, lively game that isn't too racy or revealing about the bride and her past.

 ## FABULOUS BRIDAL QUIZ

Since this creative game puts the bride in the spotlight, everyone can be an expert, and anyone can win! Whether the vibe at your party is slightly sexy, surprisingly quirky, or sweetly tame, you can tailor the questions on this quiz to fit your crowd. Guarantees a great time for groups of any size!

❋ **Prep Work:** Download our cute quiz template at www.chroniclebooks.com/bridesmaidguide. Or type up the quiz on your computer. Print and make enough copies to distribute to all your guests. (Bonus: This is easy to assemble at work!) Collect plenty of pencils and pens to hand out at the party.

THE BRIDE [insert name] **AND GROOM** [insert name] **TRIVIA CHALLENGE**
Please circle one answer only per question.

Sample questions and answers:

Where were the bride and groom when he proposed?

a. In Tuscany

b. Stuck in traffic

c. At home on the sofa

How long did the bride and groom know each other before they became engaged?

a. Since dinosaurs ruled the Earth

b. Two years

c. Six months

What's the bride's biggest pet peeve about the groom?

a. His hobby of building beer-can pyramids in his underwear

b. His refusal to wear underwear

c. His style of dress

Is the bride a natural blonde? (circle one)

Yes   No

Other sample questions:

What's the groom's middle name?

How did these two lovebirds meet?

What does the bride think is the groom's best feature?

Where did the groom grow up?

✴ **Helpful Hints:** The questions and answers can be as earnest, playful, or naughty as you want—as long as the sensibility is in step with the bride's. Creating a personalized quiz will not only make everyone laugh, but also make the bride feel special. Asking questions that are open for interpretation—like whether or not she is a natural blonde, even if her bought-and-paid-for highlights are common knowledge—makes reading out the answers even more fun. (With this question in particular, the guests often split into camps, with the bride's loyal friends backing up her natural-blonde status, and the older crowd laughing and taking the opposite position.) When crafting your quiz, be sure to consider the feelings of any older relatives or family friends who might be in attendance. Try to come up with ten to fifteen questions and answers.

✳ **How to Play:** Print out the quiz and make copies to distribute at the shower (try playful pink or floral-edged paper). Give everyone a few minutes to respond to the questions—but not so long that people start exchanging answers! If there is a tie, the bride can read off bonus questions that you've prepared especially for this scenario. Be sure the bonus round includes some zingers—everyone likes to see the bride blush. When a winner is selected, she (or he) gets to choose a gift from the basket of favors.

✳ **Easy Adaptation:** For a Jack-and-Jill shower, make different quizzes—one for the bride and one for the groom. On the bride's version, ask questions about the groom or about men in general; on the groom's quiz, ask questions about the bride or women in general. Then divide the guests into male and female teams. The women try to guess how the groom responded to the questions, and the men try to guess the bride's answers. When the teams are finished, the bride and groom—who should complete their respective quizzes separately, before the party begins—reveal their answers. Whichever guest came closest to the couple's real answers wins a prize.

PLANT THE KISS ON THE HOTTIE

This girly and grown-up version of Pin the Tail on the Donkey involves a blindfold and lipstick kisses planted on the bride's favorite TV, movie, or literary celebrity. Lively enough to keep mischievous bridesmaids happy, yet chaste enough to be enjoyed by grandmothers and aunts, this funny and festive game is a crowd-pleaser.

✳ **Prep Work:** Locate photographs or drawings of the man in question. Surprise the bride with a little creativity. If she's a closet vampire fiend, go with *Twilight*'s Edward Cullen. Is she a lit major who loves classics? Pick Mr. Darcy from *Pride and Prejudice*. From rugged sports players to bad-boy rappers to indie rock stars, there has to be someone—besides her fiancé—who strikes her fancy. Once you find the image online, print out the photographs and make at least one hundred copies. (Don't worry if the quality is terrible! That really isn't the point.) If her dream stud's likeness is unavailable, trace a life-size figure on a roll of butcher paper, cut it out with scissors, and write his name at the top. Pick up a bunch of 99-cent lipsticks in dark shades so each girl gets her own, and bring a scarf or bandana to the party to use as a blindfold.

In a room of the apartment or house where the party will happen, tape the copied photographs of the stud in question on the walls and doors. At least one wall should be completely papered over with his image. When you usher the bride-to-be inside, be prepared to bolster her with a drink—she might feel weak at the sight of so much masculine beauty!

✱ **How to Play:** Any guest can go first. Have her apply a thick coat of lipstick, and then blindfold her with the scarf or bandana. As in Pin the Tail on the Donkey, turn her in a circle three times in one direction, and three times in the other. Then turn her so she's facing the wall papered over with the images of her celebrity, and give her a gentle nudge in the right direction.

The object of the game is for her to kiss the picture on the lips—the winner is the guest who leaves her mark closest to the correct area. Of course, you can also give a second prize for the kiss that lands in the most creative spot.

TWO TRUTHS AND A LIE (A BRIDE-CENTRIC VERSION)

This old favorite becomes excellent fun when given the right bridal shower spin, and it breaks the ice better than any game around. Plus, the guests do the creative work, so the hostess is off the hook.

✱ **Prep Work:** A few days before the party, send an e-mail to guests asking them to brainstorm three statements about the bride—two should be true, and one should be false. The idea is to make it difficult for other guests to discern which is fact and which is fiction. For example:

"Susan played the tuba for a year in high school."

"Susan is marrying a man who wears his socks to bed."

"Susan once drank three shots of tequila and streaked across her college quad on a dare."

Encourage guests to include funny and interesting tidbits from the bride's past, like the perm that turned her hair green or the disastrous dinner she cooked for a date. The more outrageous the true statements are, the harder it will be for guests to identify the lie. (If you forget to ask guests to prepare in advance, don't fret—this game works well on the spur of the moment, too.)

✳ **How to Play:** Have guests sit in a circle. Choose one guest to start things off by telling her two truths and a lie. After her statements have been made, the speaker and the bride keep quiet while the other guests speculate—"Would she really have done that?" The bride gets to listen to the debate, and hilarity always ensues. Everyone in the group then votes on a slip of paper for the statement they believe is the lie. (In small groups, you can vote by raising hands.) Finally, after the votes have been tallied and the results have been announced, the bride reveals the truth! If the speaker lied convincingly enough to get everyone to vote for her lie, she wins a gift from the basket of favors. Move on to the next guest until everyone has had her turn.

FABULOUS TIP ⟫⟫→

THE GAME TO STAY AWAY FROM

The traditional Clothespin Game in which every guest wears a clothespin until they screw up by saying the forbidden word—usually *wedding*—remains mysteriously popular despite being rather tedious. The truth is, any fabulous bridesmaid will say the forbidden word right off, just to get that pesky clothespin off her outfit. Skip this dull game in favor of something more inventive.

TRADITIONAL GAMES

Sometimes you want to stick with what's tried and true. Here are a few of the most amusing time-honored shower game favorites.

RIBBON BOUQUET

This tradition will charm the older folks in the crowd, although it's more of a one-person activity than a game. Using the ribbons from the shower gifts, a bridesmaid creates a mock bouquet by threading the ribbons through a hole in a paper-plate base. According to tradition, the ribbons represent the bride's fertility—the more ribbons, the more children she will have. (With the number of gifts at showers these days, let's hope nobody actually ends up with a kid for every ribbon!) The bride can carry the mock bouquet at the wedding rehearsal or simply keep it as a piece of memorabilia.

WEDDING NIGHT PREVIEW

While the bride opens her gifts, a bridesmaid secretly writes down all the bride's exclamations. For example, "I know just where to put these!" or "Can you show me how this works?" When all the gifts have been opened, the mischievous maid will come forward and read the bride's comments aloud, describing them as the words of passion she will spout on her wedding night.

PURSE RAID

This easy game works for crowds of all ages. In advance, brainstorm a long list of objects that might be found in the purses of the guests. Start with the obvious, move on to the personal, and then go for all-out wacky. The game leader calls out the list, and the first guest to produce an item from her bag wins her pick from a basket of small favors. The master list might include items such as lipstick, state quarter, Altoids, expired coupon, digital photo of the bride, ten-dollar bill, pink (or silver or green) credit card, nail polish, prescription pills, ibuprofen, pepper spray, and temporary tattoos.

TOILET PAPER BRIDE

It's not especially eco-friendly nor will it make guests look elegant, but people still love this game and its hilarious photo opportunities. To play, divide the shower guests into groups of six or fewer, and put the groups in different rooms. Give each group several rolls of toilet paper, several white garbage bags, and a few paper clips. One person from each group is the model—mothers or mothers-in-law make excellent ones—and other team members dress her in a bridal gown, fashioning it from the materials they've been given (no tape or scissors allowed). The bride gets to wander around and watch the festivities, judge the final fashion show, and pick the winner, who gets a small prize. Don't forget to designate one person to snap pictures.

4

THE
BACHELORETTE
PARTY

Golden Rules

The bachelorette party—a treasured chance for the bride to bond with her girls and blow off steam—is usually held in the month before the wedding. This section includes everything you'll need to pull off the event, whether you're looking for ideas for easy themes, naughty games, group gifts, or special ways to personalize the party. A little planning and organization are required, but above all, this event is about fun. Take these golden rules to heart and you'll end up with a party that is both frivolous and unforgettable.

DO IT!

When both bride-love and budget have been challenged by dress buying, shower hosting, and emotional crisis counseling—and the big day is just weeks away—some bridesmaids have been known to wonder whether the bachelorette party is really necessary. In fact, few things are more essential! No polite gift-opening gabfest can replace the bachelorette bash, for the bride or the bridesmaids. This party is the bride's singleton swan song, her absolute last chance to celebrate the end of an era—and every bride deserves one.

BRING SEXY BACK

If you think bachelorette parties have to be crass, think again. (Of course, if the bride has hinted she's always wanted to see a nude male revue, then you know what to do!) Sexing things up is part of the point, but that doesn't mean male strippers are required. If X-rated activities aren't her style, have a makeup tutorial on smoky bedroom eyes or buy her satin sheets. You know the bride's tastes and preferences, so use it to your advantage, and bring sexy back in a way she'll enjoy.

MAKE A SPECTACLE

Finding little ways to embarrass the bride is a fun part of bachelorette tradition. But making her blush doesn't have to mean a lap dance. (All it takes to make some brides-to-be squirm is to doll them up in bright blue eye shadow and a Bumpit for their spa check-in.) Go for good-natured teasing that appeals to the bride's sense of humor. Perennial favorite ways to abash the bride include dressing her up in a cheesy bridal veil, cheap feather boa, or

sparkly tiara, then taking her out on the town. Make a production over her in public. After all, she asked to be in the spotlight by deciding to go through with this matrimonial madness—so let her have it!

GET WHAT YOU PAY FOR

If you and the other bridesmaids plan to host a party at a bar or restaurant that you're not completely familiar with, send a scout to sample the atmosphere, food, and drink. That way you can ensure that the spot is good, and get a solid idea of the prices. The same goes for hiring "talent" for a party—don't just call any astrologer you find online—do the research to find someone great.

DON'T HAVE THE BACHELORETTE PARTY THE NIGHT BEFORE THE WEDDING

Attending the rehearsal dinner and trying to get a good night's sleep are the only events the bride should tackle the evening before her ceremony. Avoid the temptation to hold the bachelorette party that night, even though it might seem convenient since everyone will be gathered together. Not only will carefree celebration be difficult to achieve in the nervous anticipation of the next day's events, any trace of a hangover the following morning will be a bummer. If the only feasible time for all-girl bonding is right before the wedding, have all the girls arrive a day early and celebrate before the twenty-four-hour countdown to the Big Day begins.

Bachelorette Party Q&A

Key questions about bachelorette-party protocol are answered here—follow these tips, and you'll avoid stepping on anyone's toes in the planning process.

Who Hosts? Any good friend of the bride's can organize this event, although usually a bridesmaid or the maid of honor gets the ball rolling. (Read: If the wedding is a month away and nobody has mentioned it, planning the party is your new assignment.) This party is all about group effort, so be sure to welcome others' opinions. If one of the bridesmaids worries that your boisterous party plan won't hit the right note with the bride, take her seriously and change the itinerary if necessary.

Who Pays? The costs are split evenly among the bridesmaids or all the guests. (If close friends of the bride who are not in the wedding party attend, they should also chip in.) Appoint the maid of honor or a bridesmaid to organize the finances and project costs so everyone contributes equally and guests know the contribution amount in advance. You may want to include the cost of a group gift in the budget.

Who's Invited? The guest list is at the bride's discretion, so consult with her closely. Invitations may be restricted to the bridal party but more often include other close friends or coworkers of the bride. Depending on her wishes, the groom's sister and other important female wedding guests—for example, the best man's significant other—may also be invited. Ideally, however, the guest list will be under a dozen and include only peers (not older relatives) who know the bride super well.

Choosing a Theme

As with planning a bridal shower, choosing a theme makes it easier to organize and pull off a fabulous bachelorette party. This section includes fun themes organized by location—so whether you plan to hit the town, take a trip, or stay home for some quality time, you'll find ideas and inspiration.

ON-THE-TOWN THEMES

A bachelorette party on the town makes the same impression on a run-of-the-mill bar as would an asteroid hitting Earth—there's a just-burned-through-the-atmosphere force field around these girls, and they always leave a memorable impression! The point of taking your bachelorette party to the streets isn't simply to party; it's to create a spectacle. Whether you stick to the classic night-out routine or throw a curve ball by suggesting some of these creative ideas, hitting the town with the ladies rocks!

FEARLESS LADIES PARTY

The bride will be amazed when you let her out of the car at a trapeze studio! Most major cities have training studios for circus performers, and their classes offer a great opportunity for all-girl bonding. Indoor rock climbing is another excellent option, and climbing gyms have guides to show you the ropes (ask if they offer discounts for large beginner groups). Kickboxing can fit the bill if your guests prefer to keep their feet on the ground. Once the endorphin rush kicks in, your bachelorettes will be

celebrating in style! Reward all that hard work with an indulgent night of decadent cocktails and a sumptuous dinner. There are also other sporting options if the bride's tastes are slightly less extreme. Cool retro bowling alleys are found in most cities these days complete with a jukebox, a cocktail lounge, and plenty of space to whoop it up (she'll look divine in a wedding veil and bowling shoes). Whether the ladies lace up their skates (at an ice rink or even an old-fashioned roller rink if you can find one) or shoot some pool, this party theme will bring out everyone's playful side.

JENNY'S TEN STOP

This party fits the bill when the bride has tons of friends, wants all of them to celebrate with her, and has serious party stamina—the Ten Stop involves hitting ten bars in ten hours. The most convenient running time is from 4 P.M. to 2 A.M. Invitations should have a clearly marked map on the back so that guests who can't stay the whole time can pop in at that hour's bar for a quick drink or dance and offer congratulations to the bride-to-be. This party is an excellent option when you're having trouble finding a time that works for everyone, since nearly all the guests will be able to squeeze in at least a short visit at some point during the night. Include one or two fun restaurants on the itinerary, so guests aren't drinking for hours on empty stomachs, and a couple of dance spots where everyone can boogie down. (Of course, remember to swap in the name of the bride before the words *Ten Stop* on the invitation, or everyone will wonder who Jenny is, and why she didn't come.)

ULTIMATE SPA DAY

Girl bonding in volcanic mud baths, bachelorette giggles in the steam room, and marvelous manicures all around…hitting the spa with the ladies makes for one fabulous party! Do your research, and make reservations according to what the bride and company prefer and can afford. Particularly if the group chips in to buy the bride's treatment in addition to paying for their own, each individual's cost will be considerable. In many cities, international neighborhoods offer options like Japanese baths or Korean spas, which are often less expensive than swanky downtown spots. Inquire about group activities when you're calling around. Many places are willing to seat friends together for mud baths or manicures so you can chat while receiving luxury treatments. (Some will even let you sneak in champagne.)

THE WORD ALERT: *SHOOTER*

A shooter is a strong drink, usually served in a shot glass, which is tossed back quickly instead of being sipped like a regular cocktail. It combines spirits, liqueurs, and nonalcoholic mixers, whereas shots only contain ingredients that are alcoholic—not that you'll be making such fine distinctions when that tray of shot glasses is delivered to your table. ✳**USAGE:** The bartender says, ***"Okay, ladies, are you ready for a round of shooters?"***

DESTINATION THEMES

Destination bachelorette parties are increasingly common—and it's not unheard of for a bride to request one outright. Such occasions present a financial challenge, since the extended party will require more than just petty cash on your part: plane tickets, hotel stays, entertainment, and meals can really add up. Smart savings here are the key. Find out if there's a family vacation house that's available or choose a destination you can drive to. Take a clear-eyed look at your bank account. If you absolutely can't afford to go, tactfully discuss it with the bride as soon as you hear about the plan; if she's a good friend, she should understand your situation. Such an occasion is not worth going broke for. However, it is worth a little financial stretch. For a tight-knit group of girlfriends, it's a chance for some fabulous good times. And as hard as this is to imagine, once everyone is married with children, these getaway opportunities are incredibly hard to come by.

SIN IN THE CITY

Nothing spells *d-e-b-a-u-c-h-e-r-y* better than a bachelorette party in a glitzy metropolitan area—so whether your bride prefers Manhattan or Miami, L.A. or Las Vegas, this urban getaway is all about glamour. You can have fun getting there, too—just don't party so hard on the plane that you have a hangover upon arrival. Outfit your crew with something fun, like specially designed matching baby tees, or bright feather boas; costumes might seem silly at home, but in foreign territory, they are the spice of life! You can book hotels and flights for reasonable rates if you reserve in advance, but this hot party option will never be cheap, so make sure all the bridesmaids are cool with the idea before making plans.

TIME CAPSULE WEEKEND

Visit the bride's old stomping grounds! Create an itinerary designed to help her remember her roots. For example, you might start at the dive hot dog stand near her college campus (the bride's favorite spot for late-night binge fests), move to the bar where she waitressed her senior year, then stop by somewhere she frequented, like the school football stadium or the dusty old library, and sneak inside to toss back a beer. After that, take it up a notch by taking a limo to that fancy bar where she went on her first date with her groom (if she knew him in college). Of course, include a side trip to that dive bar or dance club where she once kissed a stranger (or a few), just to remind her of her sketchy past. End the day with a slumber party on the floor of an apartment or hotel suite. The next morning, take a long walk before stopping at her favorite scenic spot for a casual brunch with mimosas and bagels, where everyone can make meaningful toasts about the next chapter in her life. The experience will be unforgettable, and the detailed itinerary itself—which will include the reason you're stopping at each place—will make an excellent keepsake for the bride.

 ## HOUSE PARTY THEMES

House parties are the best way to be fabulous on a budget, since you control the expenses—and you can decide in advance where to splurge and where to save. Plus, your bridal party can bond better without the interruptions of bar crowds and noise. Give in to the temptation to stay at home with the girls! When you host one of the following parties, the bride will be blown away by your creativity and class, and your bank account won't go bust.

ASTROLOGY EVENT

Yes, astrologers do house calls—and hiring talent can be affordable when the total cost is shared among the guests! Consult with the bridesmaids before procuring a professional and making a financial commitment. Changing the date at the last minute or having only half of the guests show up can result in a minor debacle, since the talent will still need to be paid in full. Astrologers aren't the only groovy types for hire—see below for even more ideas. Create menus, decorations, and drinks inspired by the evening's entertainment to put the finishing touches on this fun and festive theme.

* **Gypsy Gathering:** Instead of an astrologer, hire a fortune teller or tarot card reader. Get the bride a full thirty-minute reading, and schedule the other guests for quick ten-minute sessions. Dim the lights, drape tapestries over the furniture, play some old Stevie Nicks, and burn some incense while you channel spirits and see into the future.

* **Swedish Massage Soiree:** Hire a masseuse who makes house calls and travels with her own portable massage chair or table. Complete the party by offering moisturizing facial masques and sliced cucumbers as eye refreshers, lighting scented candles, and serving invigorating drinks and healthful snacks. (Bloody Marys can be both at once!)

* **Henna Tattoo Night:** Hire an expert in this ancient art to adorn the hands and feet of the guests with intricate, gorgeous, and delicate tattoos. In traditional Indian custom, this beautification routine is performed on brides the night before their wedding, but here, the bridesmaids get the benefits, too! The temporary henna designs should wash off in several days, so they'll be gone before the ceremony if you hold your party weeks in advance. Be sure to have cameras on hand to capture the impressive designs.

RITE OF PASSAGE REVEL

The highly noble goal of this funny, faux New Age party—which includes an Ex-Boyfriend Exorcism and a Karaoke Cleanse—is to purify the bride's checkered past so she can get married with a clean slate. Whip up some healthful and refreshing drinks and let the purifications begin (wheatgrass shots optional).

Ex-Boyfriend Exorcism

* **Step One:** Appoint a mistress of ceremonies to take charge of the exorcism. Any bridesmaid or maid of honor can play this part, so long as she's willing to wear a black witchy gown or some sort of mystical headdress. The bride and other ladies gather in a circle—the "Circle of Power"—while the mistress of ceremonies performs the ceremonial

lighting of the sage. (Use a dried herb bundle and light until it just begins to smolder, or opt for sage incense instead.)

✳ **Step Two:** Once the bouquet begins to let off its potent, magical smoke, the mistress of ceremonies should gesture to the north, south, east, and west, intoning, "Through the ages, sage has been used to cleanse and renew the spirit, and we now call upon its special power to exorcise the spirits of the bride's ex-boyfriends." She can use these exact words, or she can make up something on the spot. But she shouldn't laugh! Ex-boyfriend exorcisms are very serious business.

✳ **Step Three:** The mistress of ceremonies will then clearly state the name of the first ex-boyfriend, along with some identifying details— so the spirits will know who he is for sure. For example, she might say, "John, the least talented guitar player in the world, may your spirit

be gone!" The Circle of Power will then repeat in unison, "John, be gone!"

✳ **Special Note:** If your group happens to have access to a fireplace or can find an open space to start a campfire, conduct the exorcism there. The spirits prefer it.

Karaoke Cleanse

Before the bride joins her music collection everlastingly with his, and she embarks on a mature, married life of shared song listening, going through this rite of passage is essential. Many brides have a lifetime of bad songs to get out of their systems! A karaoke-based sing-along video game works perfectly if you have access to a Nintendo Wii system or something similar. Make sure it includes a long list of chart-topping songs so her faves will be included. Or take the tried-and-true option and rent an actual karaoke machine. At the party, the bride has to belt out all her old favorites. Not one drippingly sentimental ballad or cheesy pop song from her youth should escape your playlist. (The printed inventory will be a treasured memento of her lifetime of musical gaffes!) Guests must join her at the microphone if she calls them up. Making a bootleg video of the occasion is highly recommended.

STORYBOOK SOIRÉE

Is there a dog-eared novel on her shelf that she reads over and over again? A TV show she won't miss unless the sky is falling? A movie she never tires of seeing? Let the story be the premise for your party: Dress the bride like her favorite heroine, serve the appropriate foods, and design the decorations and games around the plot. A few ideas:

* **Undying Love:** From *True Blood* to *Twilight*, lots of ladies these days are seeing red. Supply guests with fake vampire teeth, make red velvet cupcakes, serve cranberry-colored drinks, and plan a game of Plant the Kiss on the Hottie (page 80) starring the bride's favorite blood-sucking fiend.

* **Make Beautiful Music:** Whether she's addicted to song-centered TV shows like *American Idol* or *Glee* or just can't get enough of Broadway musicals, key your affair around music to remember. Rewrite the lyrics to one of the bride's favorite songs and hand them out for a performance once she arrives—you could even have the group practice in advance.

* **Classic Courtship:** The first line of Jane Austen's *Pride and Prejudice* provides a timeless wedding theme: "It is a truth universally acknowledged that a single man in possession of a good fortune must be in want of a wife." If the bride loves this book or one of its many film adaptations, consider an event inspired by nineteenth-century passions. Serve an old-fashioned buffet, play a quaint game of cards, and offer read-aloud entertainment (for example, your list of "The Top Ten Ways the Groom Is Like Mr. Darcy").

SPA PARTY

Create a "spa studio" in your home and bring the bridal party together for an afternoon of healing tea, hot foot soaks, and pedicures. Create a comfortable sitting area, crank up the thermostat, and play a soundtrack of ocean waves and bird songs. Burn candles or sandalwood incense, and dim the lights. Handwrite a Spa Studio sign for the door of the room, so guests have the experience of entering a separate, specifically calming place; on the sign, include a reminder to turn off cell phones. Ask your guests to bring or wear loose, comfortable clothing. As hostess, have everything set up before guests arrive, so you can stay relaxed yourself. Some ideas:

❋ Create a relaxing custom mix of whole tea leaves for the bride at a natural food store or tea shop. Think about what healing she might need: Chamomile promotes relaxation, while peppermint invigorates. Ginseng energizes, while calendula heals.

❋ Set up a simple table where you offer steaming tea with honey and wedges of lemon in Japanese-style ceramic teacups and serve healthful foods like dried fruit and raw almonds in wooden bowls.

❋ As favors, give jars of the loose-leaf tea (create handmade labels using wedding bells cut from construction paper) and name it for the bride—say, Samantha's Stress Soother.

❋ Set up an aromatic foot soak for each guest. Purchase individual plastic basins and new white hand towels in advance (both items should be cheap and easy to find at a store like Target). Prepare each foot bath with steaming water and add a few drops of essential oil—try tangerine or eucalyptus to invigorate or lavender or sandalwood to soothe.

❋ Have key nail tools on hand so anyone who wants to can do her pedicure, including cute extras like toe separators and refreshing peppermint foot lotion. Supply a handful of adorable polish colors or ask each guest to contribute a bottle in her favorite hue.

Party Planning Guidelines

The bachelorette party won't require as much formal planning as a bridal shower, but advance organization is still the key to success. If you are planning a simple and straightforward night out with the girls, follow the four simple steps below to get the ball rolling. If the event is a destination bachelorette party, or involves multiple reservations and lots of guests, refer to the more detailed steps in A Shower Planning Checklist (page 76).

* **Finalize the theme and venue.** After consultation with your guests for ideas, finalize the theme and venue. As ideas emerge, keep in mind what the ballpark budget might be. A clear-eyed look at the finances might change your mind about what type of event to have; a house party will cost less than a day at an opulent spa.

* **Finalize the date.** Coordinating the schedules of a bunch of girls on the go can take weeks. Start nailing down the date as soon as possible, preferably at least two months before the wedding, since some friends may fly into town for the occasion. Use Doodle to organize schedules.

* **Broadcast the budget.** The party hinges on everyone contributing their fair share, so start the money conversation well in advance of the event. Send a friendly e-mail to everyone who will attend. "I know we're all looking forward to our celebration of Anne in a couple of weeks! The advance party squad will meet at Landmark Tavern on Friday at 5:30. Dinner is fixed-price ($55) plus tax and tip (cash, please) plus any booze you choose to drink, with all six of us chipping in an extra $15 each to cover Anne's meal and cocktails. After dinner, we'll head out for further libations." This way, if anyone has problems with the money situation or the plan, you can address them early so the night itself goes smoothly.

* **Send the invitations.** Group e-mails or online invites work well for this casual occasion. Sending paper invitations isn't necessary, but they are charming and always welcome (download our bachelorette invitation templates at www.chroniclebooks .com/bridesmaidguide). For simplicity and an easy way to keep track of who can come, Evite always works, or you can opt to send a pretty electronic invitation through a service like Paperless Post (www .paperlesspost.com). Keep this in mind: If you don't hear back from someone promptly, it's possible your invite went straight to their spam box, so follow up with a phone call.

- Have a few rowdy rounds of cocktails and games at home before you hit the bar circuit.

- Prepare the hors d'oeuvres yourself, or with the other bridesmaids, instead of hiring caterers.

- If your party hits the town, choose a lively neighborhood with plenty of hot spots, so you can barhop on foot instead of spending a fortune on taxis.

- If you're having a house party, keep the food and decorations simple, and save your money for fun gifts and good booze.

- Get creative with your games and decorations and make them yourself—no need to buy them unless you're really pressed for time.

- Whatever embarrassing garment you're going to make the bride wear in public—a bonnet, a feather boa, or a tiara, for example—find it or make it in advance. The joke will be on you if you have to spend a fortune and pay for next-day shipping to get the item in question.

Headpiece and X-Rated Extras

Once you've chosen a theme, finalized the date, projected your budget, and gotten all the guests on board, all that remains is to line up the games and essential extras to give your bachelorette plenty of personality. For everything you need, consider something like *The Bachelorette Party Kit* (find it at www.amazon.com)—it comes complete with sparkly tiara, naughty dice game, and more. Or, use this list as your template for key party starters.

✳ **Headpiece for the bride:** (We can't repeat this enough.) Sure, a small veil works, but so do tiaras and wigs and unusual hats. Choose something that will make the bride cringe just a little bit.

✳ **Sex-themed accessories:** For a creative touch, we like naughty temporary tattoos or specially designed T-shirts ("Sex Kitten"). Predictable yet embarrassing extras like penis straws remain a staple (and a lot easier to handle than a male stripper who turns out to be super sleazy).

* **Bride-centered games:** Set the tone and remind everyone this isn't just a party—it's the bride's party—by having guests take the "Bride's Dark Secrets" Quiz (page 103) or contribute to a Snapshot Time Line (see facing page) before you head out for cocktails.

* **Digital camera:** Consider using one designated camera that you pass between bridesmaids so one person isn't stuck playing shutterbug all night. Then you'll have all the shots in one place. If lots of people have cameras, a gentle reminder not to post or tag photos of the bride in compromising positions might be appropriate. After the party, if the bride agrees, post the pictures to a photo-sharing site, like Flickr or Shutterfly, where everyone can relive the good times (but her boss who friended her on Facebook won't see them).

Gift Suggestions

Presents aren't as important at the bachelorette party as they are at the shower—after all, each person is already paying for her share of the party's bottom line. That said, this occasion is the perfect time to give funny and personal gifts, and not just the kind that cost money, either. While the group may want to chip in to get the bride something naughty, crafting something creative in addition will go a long way toward making the evening special. Brainstorm with the bridesmaids to decide on the memento that will best capture the moment. The ideas listed below include some items that can be found in stores, and others that are meaningful, nostalgic gifts that only best friends can give. When the whole group shares the burden of effort and expense, it is easy to offer her both types of presents— the material and the more sentimental— while keeping costs low.

CLASSIC BACHELORETTE GIFTS

A blue garter that the bride can wear at her wedding is one traditional offering (it can function as the blue element of the "something old, new, borrowed, and blue" good-luck charm). Lingerie of any type is also a classic gift, especially gorgeous, expensive, slinky items that a practical bride might not purchase for herself. Frivolous bedroom accessories or sex toys are another option (if the bride appreciates this type of present). All these items make excellent group gifts, but you can't just assume everyone will chip in—instead, e-mail the bridesmaids before you buy the gift and get their approval for the type of item and price range you have in mind.

Gift certificates are also a good bet because of their flexibility—you can give her a lavish spa treatment or an indulgent massage. Another option is a certificate for a meal for two at her favorite restaurant. Theater tickets—or, if you want to splurge, a night at a romantic bed-and-breakfast—are also extremely thoughtful gifts. The wedding couple will probably be strapped for cash when they return from their honeymoon, and this way, romantic dinners and getaways won't be out of the question.

HANDCRAFTED BACHELORETTE GIFTS

Snapshot Time Line

Have every bridesmaid go through the old photographs she has of the bride and herself and pick out those that have special significance. Ask the ladies to show up at the party early, and collaborate to make a time line on butcher paper. Tape the photographs to the paper in chronological order, and write captions beneath each describing that moment in the bride's life. The chronology can include typical "big moments," like birthdays or graduations, or it can be more tongue-in-cheek. If you have a photograph of her from junior high with bad hair, for example, pin up the image with a caption that describes this moment as her worst bad-hair day. The quirkier your photos and captions, the funnier the time line will be. You can also include photographs that commemorate when she met each of the bridesmaids.

Farrah Fawcett meets Chewbacca

Depending on how long her bridesmaids have known her, the time line can begin at infancy, or start later, perhaps during her college years. Whether the time line is sentimental or sassy, this gift is something she can fold up and treasure forever.

Friendship Book

Get a nice blank journal, and have every guest decorate a page or two, with anything from photographs and ticket stubs to poems and recipes, and dust the pages with glitter or adorn them with gold stars. Each of the entries will be unique and represent the particular kind of friendship that person shares with the bride. Somewhere on the page, each guest must include some piece of advice for the bride as she starts her new life. Ask the groom to contribute a page as well—he's likely to write incredibly sweet and earnest things. On the front of the book, create a colorful collage of favorite photographs of the bride and the friends who attend the bachelorette party. This gift is guaranteed to be tearjerker as the bride pages through the book and sees how much she is loved.

Best Bachelorette Games

Candy necklaces aren't the only game in town. Do a little advance planning and make the most of the bride's naughty side by planning ahead; ask the guests to take the "Bride's Dark Secrets" Quiz (facing page) or create a sassy Bachelorette Scavenger Hunt. Whatever the competition, consider bringing along a few brightly wrapped favors to reward the winners. Small X-rated prizes (think Astroglide or scented massage lotion) are both naughty and nice.

BACHELORETTE SCAVENGER HUNT

✳ **Easy Concept:** This fun game, originally published in *The Bachelorette Party Kit* (also from Chronicle Books), is easy to play at the bride's favorite cocktail bar. You could also expand the field of play to an eight- or four-block area, if you're in a good walking neighborhood with a concentration of nightclubs and cocktail bars. Have bachelorettes pair up or get into small groups (use that old gym class trick where each person calls out "one" or "two" to split the guests into two evenly sized teams).

* **Prep Work:** Visit www.chronicle books.com/bridesmaidguide for our downloadable scavenger hunt template. Print out the number of copies you will need (a few extras are always a good idea) and bring them with you to the party. Don't forget a cache of chic glitter pens! Alternately, just type up your own list and include the following items:

Cocktail napkin with a guy's number on it

Label from a pair of boxer shorts

A digital photo of great bar bathroom graffiti

Picture of a shirtless guy torn from a free weekly newspaper

A business card from a married man

Drink coaster with lipstick kiss from an unmarried woman

Condom or sex toy from bathroom dispenser

A cigarette from a single guy

Bartender's recipe for a Blow Job shot

* **How to Play**: Give a sheet of hunt items to each team. Synchronize cell phone clocks and agree on a central meeting place where the teams will converge once the hunt is finished. Assign a time deadline: If the field of play is a single bar, set the deadline for twenty or thirty minutes; if it's larger, make it forty-five minutes or an hour. Teams *must* return to the central meeting place when the time deadline expires. Actual items such as the boxer shorts label and the married man's business card must be physically submitted for credit. Other items, such as the phrase of bathroom graffiti and a bartender's recipe for a Blow Job shot, can be documented in a photo, recited, or displayed in written form. Whichever team successfully checks off the most categories by the deadline is the winning team. The losers must buy the winners Blow Job shots. If it's a tie, everyone wins—Blow Job shots all around!

* **Note:** bring a glue stick and mini keepsake album so you can paste the scavenger hunt paraphernalia into a keepsake album for the bride!

 ## "BRIDE'S DARK SECRETS" QUIZ

Whether you're waiting for your first round of cocktails or welcoming everyone to your at-home event, hand out this funny quiz about the bride to break the ice. Use our Fabulous Bridal Quiz (page 78) as a template, but change the questions so the quiz becomes a daring tell-all about the

bride instead of a polite shower pastime. Write questions that focus on her wild past, including her junior high mishaps, funny dating faux pas, and legendary college exploits. For example: In her first college experience drinking tequila, where did the bride sustain an injury? Answers: (a) Her knee (b) Her tongue (c) Her pride. Whichever bachelorette answers the most questions correctly wins a prize.

The Wedding Countdown

The bachelorette party takes place around the same time that you'll want to finalize the last details for attending the wedding itself. Who will you bring? Where will you stay? What will you pack? These details can make or break your weekend, so use this savvy advice to make smart decisions.

 ## WHERE TO STAY

A bridesmaid's bedroom or hotel room is her beautification center and her headquarters for hangover healing. Unfortunately, decent lodging doesn't come cheap, but be honest with yourself about where you will feel comfortable staying. Doing some minor damage to your bank account is worth it when your sanity hangs in the balance. Review these handy lists of lodging options before you take the reservation plunge, and then choose the place where you'll wake up feeling bold, beautiful, righteous, relaxed, and ready to party!

LUXURY HOTEL

Pros	*Cons*
✻ Private and reasonably quiet	✻ High-priced rooms
✻ Giant bed great for slumber parties	✻ Hotel staff more beautiful than you
✻ Hotel bar	✻ Proximity of hotel bar and giant bed potentially dangerous
✻ Spa and sauna	
✻ Room cleaning/room service	✻ Busy schedule means no time for spa

ADVICE: Share with other bridesmaids to bring down the cost.

CLASSY BED-AND-BREAKFAST

Pros

* Pleasant, homey atmosphere

* Quiet in the evenings

* You'll be the prettiest one staying there since all the other guests are over fifty

* Delicious breakfast included

Cons

* Lack of privacy due to paper-thin walls and nosy guests

* Noisy in the morning—the very early morning

* Unavoidable small talk with owners and other guests

* Allergens in the environment thanks to pets or ancient stuffed furniture

ADVICE: Bring allergy medication and earplugs.

CHEESY MOTEL

Pros

* Cheap rooms

* No morning small talk with other wedding guests (you'll be the only wedding guest staying there)

* Rooms always available, even when everywhere else is booked

* Rowdiness in the halls and rooms unlikely to be checked, so you could host a party

Cons

* Appearance of being financially challenged, unemployed, or both

* Scratchy polyester-blend sheets; bad fluorescent lighting in bathroom; depressing, pea-sized outdoor pool

* High likelihood that your neighbors will have loud, late-night sex

* Possibility of car getting vandalized in dimly lit parking lot

ADVICE: Keep your suitcase off the floor so you don't bring home bedbugs.

CAMPING

Pros

* Free!

* Opportunity to experience the beauty of nature

* Great excuse for not being perfectly made-up and well coiffed

* Will please your outdoorsy or budget-conscious date

Cons

* Dark under-eye circles from restless night spent listening to deer/raccoons/bears prowl around the tent

* No decent shower

* Uncomfortable sleeping arrangements preclude cuddling with outdoorsy date

* Nightlong proximity to campfires might make you a barbecue-scented bridesmaid

ADVICE: Arrange to get ready for the wedding in another bridesmaid's hotel room.

WHAT TO PACK

Now that many airlines charge a hefty fee to check your bag, the budget-conscious bridesmaid might think carry-on is the way to go for the wedding. Don't push it. If a tiny roller suitcase fits all your skincare products and shoes, that's great, but don't leave behind key beauty essentials just to save a few bucks. Here's a handy packing list to make sure you have everything you need to be physically and psychically prepared for the wedding weekend.

What to Pack

* Skincare products

...and Why

If the hotel soap gives you an all-over body rash, you'll still have to wear your sleeveless bridesmaid dress.

* Cozy pajamas

You won't get much sleep, but you can make those few hours count by being comfortable.

* Stunning rehearsal dinner outfit

This is your chance to show everyone how divine you can look when the bride isn't choosing your clothes.

* Bridesmaid dress, shoes, accessories

You have no choice.

* Great lipstick and sparkly hair accessories

They might distract people from your bad bridesmaid dress.

* Shawl or wrap

Borrowing his tuxedo jacket when it gets cold will make your outfit look even worse.

* Comfy outfit for the trip home

You'll need something stretchy to wear in the event of cake- or hangover-induced bloating.

* Satin ballet flats

Bring to reception in case your heels make you want to stop dancing early; flip-flops will also do in a pinch.

* Allergy medicine

Runny noses aren't cute.

* Ibuprofen or painkiller of choice

Unless you successfully observe wedding golden rule number three (hydrate, hydrate, hydrate), you'll need it for your hangover.

* Wedding invitation and directions

Being late or lost will ruin your cool.

* Camera

You'll want to get photos of yourself chatting with handsome, well-dressed men, or capture the image of your boyfriend all cleaned up for once.

* Emergency wedding day kit

Miniature sewing kit, lip balm, blotting sheets, bobby pins, stain treater towelettes, Band-Aids for any blisters, tissues, Q-Tips, eyedrops for taking the red out of eyes and last-minute skin flaws, extra stockings, clear nail polish, and colored nail polish to match your manicure or pedicure should you end up with an unfortunate chip.

WHO TO BRING

There are many compelling reasons to bring a date with you to a wedding. Some stem from romantic sentiments—it's nice to hold hands during those emotional speeches—while others are more practical, like needing someone to pal around with when everyone else couples up. But before you grab the first guy you see, consider the benefits of going alone—flying solo is liberating and much better than bringing an undesirable date. This goes for all ladies, married or single. A sulky boyfriend or stressed husband hanging on your arm can definitely damage your carefree state of mind. The bottom line is that you shouldn't worry about what people think about your dating status—just whether having that particular person by your side will make the evening more fun.

Another thing to consider is that you won't be able to spend much time with your date. As a bridesmaid, you will be busy at bridal headquarters— so if your companion doesn't have the energy or will to tackle the social situations alone, he or she might be better left at home! Also, if your date doesn't know the couple getting married, he or she may feel out of place at such an intimate occasion, given that you will be MIA much of the time.

The date debate is moot, however, if you are not supposed to bring anyone at all. If you are in doubt, the first place to look is the wedding invitation: your name and your steady's name (or the words "and guest") should appear on the envelope. If not, you may be expected to fly solo. Fortunately, if you have a serious, live-in significant other, this probably won't be an issue. The protocol these days is to invite significant others, and some brides even emphasize their importance by seating them with you at the bridal table. (The caring bride will call her bridesmaids in advance to confirm the spelling of the significant other's name, so it appears correctly on the invitation and place cards. If she doesn't do this, forgive her in the magnanimous spirit of bride-love.)

But what about your new crush? Again, check your invite. If it doesn't specify "and guest" or "plus one," you might be out of luck. If your date is extremely important to you, and you think the bride might be open to it, you can make the request—but know that asking her to add one more person to an already-completed guest list is not advisable. Proceed with caution.

5
THE WEDDING WEEKEND

Golden Rules

With far-flung friends and relatives flying in early, and festive dinners and intimate gatherings being held in the days before the ceremony, wedding days have become wedding weekends. Even if you live right next door to the ceremony site, your schedule in the days before the wedding will likely be jam-packed. At the very least, you will attend the rehearsal dinner the evening before the ceremony, and there may be an event to attend the day after. For a destination wedding on an exotic island or rustic farm, the time line can expand to four or five days. You'll need stamina, as well as stunning social skills, to survive the marathon in style. Follow these golden rules, and you'll give the performance of a lifetime.

BE BOLD

Once upon a time, bridesmaids just stood around looking pretty—but these days, they have to be up for a challenge! You might have to help row an outrigger canoe between tropical islands to the ceremony, or the group might be asked to wear matching outfits and ski halfway down a mountain to the wedding site. Or the reception might be so large that you feel like Evita when you give your speech onstage in front of hundreds of people. Whatever the challenge, go for the gold. You're not just a supportive friend wearing a questionable outfit—you're the bride's fellow adventurer!

LET LOVE RULE

Don't bottle up your emotions! Whether you shed tears during the ceremony or broadcast your love for the happy couple over the microphone at the reception, let your sentimental side show. Weddings are the one place where everybody gets to be as sappy, syrupy, and romantic as they want. It's beautiful. Go with it!

HYDRATE, HYDRATE, HYDRATE

Down at least one full glass of water between each festive glass of champagne or wine, and stay within your comfort zone—the sobriety level you might aim for at an office party—or, even more challenging, the level at which you'd feel comfortable chatting up a gorgeous movie star. The idea is to be dazzling, not dazed and confused.

NAIL THE TIMING

Be punctual. Being on time is one way of showing the bride—and everyone else—how much you love and respect her. Ideally, the bridesmaids will input wedding-related plans and appointments electronically into their phones or calendars so every detail is at their fingertips. Inevitably, however, one person is clueless. That's why hard-copy schedules have their place, too. If the wedding day is packed, print an itinerary on pretty paper for each bridesmaid that details the timing so everyone knows when to show up at the salon or the photo session.

OBEY THE TWENTY-FOUR-HOUR RULE

In the twenty-four-hour period preceding the wedding, insulate the bride from stress at all costs. If you are irritated or concerned about something and you feel you must get it off your chest, talk to another bridesmaid about what's eating you. Don't hassle the bride, have it out with her, or disturb her in any way once the time-honored gag rule goes into effect.

Rehearsal Dinner Dos and Don'ts

The essentials of the rehearsal and the accompanying dinner—a walk-through of the ceremony and a meal afterward—haven't changed a great deal over the decades, but the emphasis has. These days, the meal is often given more importance than the actual wedding rehearsal. The dinner has become such an important and lavish part of the wedding weekend that the hosting duties have changed hands. In the old days, the bride's family was responsible for the rehearsal dinner as well as the wedding, but more recently it has become customary for the dinner to be hosted by the groom's parents. If the evening involves dinner only, a quick rehearsal may often be held the following morning in advance of the ceremony.

Sometimes, the guest list is small enough to provide an opportunity for the bride and groom to spend quality time with their intimate circle of friends and family. Alternately, the exclusive guest list is dispensed with and everyone who arrives in town the night before the ceremony is invited. In this case, the meal is usually more casual, say, a barbecue or picnic on the beach. Follow our Dos and Don'ts, and you'll win an award for most mannerly bridesmaid.

• *Do dress appropriately.* Since this event can range from pearls-and-heels formal to shorts-and-sandals casual, do a little advance research. Also, some brides will ask the bridesmaids to buy matching dresses for the dinner (yes, in addition to their dresses for the wedding), but the majority will let you wear what you like.

• *Don't be shy.* Being a bridesmaid gives you an automatic reason to introduce yourself and break the ice with other guests. Make it your goal to find out how every person in the room knows the bride. Talk to elderly guests, children, anyone who seems shy or lonely, and, if you can, anyone who speaks another language. If there are extraterrestrials in the crowd, speak with them, too.

• *Do mind your manners.* When you're a bridesmaid, people notice you. Extended family members flying completely beneath your radar may well know your name, age, and even your dating status. Use your very best table manners, keep your conversation polite, and don't text, giggle, or whisper during the formal toasts that may be given after dinner.

- ***Don't get rip-roaring drunk.*** Imagine what might happen if you drank so much at the rehearsal dinner that your uncontrollable hangover the following day compelled you to throw up right before or during the ceremony. Then imagine that this has actually happened to more than one well-meaning bridesmaid.

- ***Do give a toast (if appropriate).*** You may see crimes of public speaking committed at this event, particularly if it's a big crowd and the host opens the floor so anyone can take the microphone. Show them the definition of classy and jump in there! The bride deserves to be represented by her best friends—that means you. Prepare in advance by checking out Spectacular Speeches and Triumphant Toasts (page 129). Even at a small dinner event, everyone around the table may be asked to say a few words, so be prepared with something funny or sentimental about the couple to share.

❗ THE WORD ALERT: *THE ROAST*

No, this is not a friendly campfire sing-along with chocolate bars and marshmallows. This is part of the speech you may be giving at any point during the wedding festivities—one designed to secure some laughs while gently skewering the bride's more "distinctive" characteristics. Go for the "PG-13" rating when you roast. Stories about her ex-boyfriends or amusing sexual exploits are definitely not appropriate. ✳ **USAGE:** The groom's father says good-naturedly, ***"I can't wait to hear you roast her!"***

Wedding Day Checklists

For every bride, no matter how formal her ceremony and reception, fun-loving bridesmaids, personal gifts, and heartfelt toasts will always be better than the stuffy versions. If the bride has an attack of stress, don't take it personally. Instead, stay organized, be resourceful, try to think of possible solutions, and keep that crucial sense of humor intact. Read on to find out what to expect as events unfold and to find helpful tips to help you sail through the big day without snags. To start, read over our must-have checklists of the wedding day duties.

CHECKLIST ONE: HOW TO BE A FABULOUS BRIDESMAID

* **Pack Up.** In the morning, pull together the makeup, hair accessories, jewelry, bridesmaid dress, and any other things you'll need in order to primp and get fabulous, then head over to bridal headquarters—usually a private room at the wedding site, or the bride's hotel suite. Maid of honor, bring that crib sheet for your toast, if you're giving one. Bring along the "something borrowed" or "something blue" for the bride, if that's your department. Stash a emergency wedding day kit in your bag (see page 107).

* **Eat and Drink.** If it seems that, between beauty appointments and other details, eating sensibly has escaped the bride's mind, figure out how to organize breakfast or lunch so nobody gets hungry. Scrambled eggs or turkey wraps will hold everyone over without making them feel bloated. Also, if the salon gives you permission to bring in a bottle of champagne, just a few sips can set the mood and make the morning feel festive (make sure the bride hydrates, too).

* **Be Beauty Savvy.** Cover your face (and the bride's) with a pillowcase when pulling the gowns over your heads so no makeup ends up where it doesn't belong. Remember that the bride should only eat before she gets dressed, so no food stains mar her gown—and the same goes for all the bridesmaids. Brush teeth before makeup application. Bring along hairpins to help with last-minute veil adjustments, as well as blotting tissues and stain treatment towelettes. Appoint a maid of honor or bridesmaid to be in charge of straightening the bride's train when she arrives at the altar so it looks smooth and flawless.

* **Handle the Bouquets.** Maid of honor, be sure the bouquets and bridesmaids are in order. Deliver corsages to the moms as needed and ditto for the groom and his attendants, if the boutonnieres are delivered to the bridal suite with the other flowers.

* **Head to the Wedding Site.** Get to the wedding site on time! Have everything ready half an hour early, whether it's your reception essentials—a cashmere wrap, lipstick, and mints—or the bride's must-have items including "something borrowed" and "something blue." Maid of honor, find out in advance when you'll take charge of the groom's ring and procure it as needed. Note: If for some reason you end up needing to dress separately and are on your own steam to get to the wedding site, arrive at least thirty minutes before the ceremony starts.

CHECKLIST TWO: HOW TO BE A FABULOUS FRIEND

Put those official duties and ceremony details aside for a moment—this little list is about making the bride feel cherished and loved! On the morning of the wedding, take a moment to appreciate your bond with the bride, and give the gift of your friendship all day long. Show the bride how much you love and appreciate her in the small ways that matter. Use these ideas for inspiration—and let your natural friendship intuition be your guide.

* Be the bride's jester, and soothe her jitters.

* Act like you know what you're doing.

* Just be around—a lot!

* Ask her if she needs anything.

* Keep her excited, and keep her smiling.

* Reassure her if she gets commitment jitters at the last minute.

* Remind her of the wonderful things about her relationship with the groom.

* Don't hate her for making you look like an overstuffed Barbie doll, or for marrying a man you think isn't perfect for her, or for anything else.

* Remember that in doing all these things, you are cementing the foundation of a wonderful lifelong friendship.

THE WORD ALERT: *IN THE RIBBONS*

This phrase has nothing to do with the bridesmaids doing a maypole dance, thankfully. In fact, it has nothing to do with bridesmaids at all—but you should know that it means a special honor section in the seating set aside for immediate family, generally the first few rows, which are traditionally marked by ribbons or bows. ✳**USAGE:** The bride's mother says, ***"Why didn't that usher seat Grandma Bessie in the ribbons?"***

SOMETHING BLUE

Even the most down-to-earth bride—the one who since girlhood has been unmoved by superstitions, astrology, or fortune-telling of all sorts—might adhere to the traditional good-luck custom of wearing "something old, something new, something borrowed, and something blue" for her wedding. And why not? This good-luck charm covers all the bases: New and old are worn together to ease the transition from the old life to the new one; the borrowed item, preferably lent by a happily married woman, is worn for good luck; and the blue item represents fidelity. Some lucky brides borrow sapphires from relatives to wear for luck, but those who don't have access to fabulous jewels will appreciate receiving a sentimental blue item from her bridesmaids as a gift. This can be given at the shower, at the bachelorette party, or even on the day of the wedding. Here are some traditional and not-so-traditional ideas:

• The classic blue garter

• Tiny blue cornflowers for the bride's hair

• Aquamarine cocktail ring

• Delicate wrist bangles

- A temporary blue tattoo (for the groom's eyes only)
- Pedicure with blue polish (hidden under closed-toe shoes)
- Blue lingerie (in a tone that won't show through the wedding dress)
- A strip of blue ribbon to pin inside the hem of her wedding gown

Getting Down the Aisle in Style

There are as many different types of weddings as there are religious beliefs, all of which have distinctive ceremonies and rites. In the United States, where Judaism, Protestantism, and Catholicism are the three most widely practiced faiths, the main events are the procession, the ceremony, and the recession. If you are involved in a wedding where the customs are unfamiliar to you, don't hesitate to admit ignorance and ask questions. The more you know about the meanings of the rituals at the wedding, the more meaningful the ceremony will be to you.

Generally, the ushers lead the procession, followed by junior ushers or junior bridesmaids, if they are in the party. Bridesmaids are next down the aisle—either walking in pairs or in single file—and the maid of honor follows. If there is a flower girl or ring bearer, she or he immediately precedes the bride, who walks accompanied by her choice of attendant (in Christian weddings, often her father; in Jewish weddings, both her father and mother). A bride may also choose to walk with another relative, such as a grandparent, or with the groom, or she may even choose to walk down the aisle alone. All these options are perfectly acceptable according to etiquette and generally won't affect the order of the bridesmaids and the maid of honor, who precede the bride in the procession.

In Jewish weddings, the rabbi waits for the bride and groom under a *huppah*, or canopy, which symbolizes the home that the couple will share. Slight variations in the order of the procession and recession and in the standing arrangements at the altar are common. To nail your role in the real event, attend the formal rehearsal, and follow these simple tips for cruising the wedding catwalk without tripping up.

FABULOUS TIP ⫸➤

HOW TO SURVIVE THE BRIDESMAID'S CATWALK

Many large wedding receptions are hosted by an official announcer (often, also the DJ) who formally introduces the attendants to the wedding crowd, just before the dinner begins. This agonizing ritual goes as follows: An announcer will say your name over the PA—your signal to take a turn on the bridesmaid's catwalk, the central reception floor—and you will walk some specified distance, perhaps wave, and even turn. In addition to letting everyone take a good gander at your bad dress, you may have to endure clapping, which can have a stinging ring of sarcasm when you're sporting a terrible outfit. How to survive? Walk as quickly as possible without tripping, and comfort yourself afterward with a glass of champagne.

HEAD DOWN THE AISLE IN STYLE

1. Maid of honor, put that precious gold circle on your thumb for safekeeping.

2. Take your place for the procession (as practiced at the rehearsal).

3. When the music or other signal is given, begin the procession. Walk slowly!

4. Fan out during the ceremony in your prearranged positions, and stay at attention.

5. Once the bride reaches the altar, if you're the maid of honor, fluff her dress and make it look pretty.

6. Maid of honor, take the bride's bouquet and offer the ring at just the right moment.

7. Keep a natural expression. Even if that baby in the crowd won't stop screaming, don't roll your eyes.

8. Hold your bouquet high. It sounds silly, but it's easy to let your arms sag and the flowers droop without noticing, especially during a long ceremony.

9. Enjoy the moment when the couple says the vows—the best part of being a bridesmaid is being close enough to see the emotions cross their faces.

10. Plan ahead and tuck a tissue or a pretty hanky into your hand holding the bridesmaid bouquet should the waterworks start. If you really lose it and start crying uncontrollably, calm down by staring lovingly at the crowd as you internally count the number of bad outfits or tacky hairdos on display.

11. Wait for the prearranged signal to start the recession down the aisle. In Jewish ceremonies, the groom crushes a wineglass beneath his feet at the end of the ceremony, directly before the recession.

Wedding Reception 101

Whether held in a backyard garden or an upscale ballroom, the reception lasts several hours at least, and usually includes dinner and dancing. It kicks off once the receiving line breaks up, or after the newlyweds have completed their happy processional from the altar. Many a bridesmaid has seized this moment to visit the restroom or take a breather, not realizing that the start of the reception means the beginning of a whole new set of duties. Read on to find out what to expect as events unfold and to get all the advice you'll need to survive the dancing, toasting, and bouquet catching in style.

✳ **Find Your Way.** If the reception will be held at a separate venue—often the case these days—don't miss your limo departure! Any delay on your part, and you might stress out the bride by arriving late to the photo session.

✳ **Say "Cheese."** Formal photographs of the couple, their families, and the wedding attendants often take place during a cocktail hour held directly after the ceremony; try not to feel too bitter that you're missing out on the drinks and hors d'oeuvres.

✳ **Take a Seat.** When the signal is given by the host or wedding planner, people will begin to find their tables. At more formal events, the newlyweds and their parents will be announced and make a grand entrance into the reception site, followed by the bridal party (escorted by groomsmen, of course).

✳ **Dine and Dance.** It used to be that the newlyweds' first dance always happened before the first course, but these days, the order of events is at the discretion of the couple or their wedding planner. Just know that at some point in the festivities, the bride and groom will share their first dance, and the wedding party will join in (look for the same partner you walked the aisle with). You'll want to take a breather to enjoy dinner and watch the special dances, such as the one between the bride and her father.

✳ **Make a Toast.** The best man usually gives the first speech, followed by the maid of honor.

✳ **Take the Cake.** The cake cutting comes at a point in the reception when even a devoted bridesmaid begins to feel off-duty—but stay in touch with what's happening, so you can applaud your dear friend when she cuts the first piece of her gorgeous wedding cake.

* **Catch the Bouquet.** If you're single, join the group for the bouquet toss. Don't hang back. Get in there!

* **Send off the Couple.** Be there when the couple makes their grand exit, and if need be, hand out favors and lend a hand wrapping up things at the reception site.

* **Hit the After-Party.** If the bride and groom can stay up another hour (or three) to celebrate, so can you, so meet them out. Besides, it's always fun to see which guests turn into train wrecks (ahem, don't let that be you).

 ## THE RECEIVING LINE

The point of this tradition is to allow each guest a chance to personally greet the bride and groom at a large and formal wedding, where they might not otherwise get face time. Whether you are standing in the line, or simply passing through it, always put down your glass or plate so you can greet people properly.

The line may take place at the church, directly after the ceremony, or form at the reception site as guests arrive for the festivities. The bride will sometimes ask her bridesmaids to stand in the line, in which case, get ready to plaster on your smile and shake lots of hands. Another task you may be assigned is to preside over the guest book, encouraging people to sign when they have finished greeting the newlyweds and the family. At small, intimate ceremonies, the receiving line is often deemed unnecessary, since the couple will presumably have a chance to speak with everyone at the reception.

 ## THE BRIDE'S TABLE

Bridesmaids always score when it comes to seating arrangements—no back-of-the-room, faraway table for you! Sometimes, the bridesmaids, ushers, and their significant others will be seated at the bride's table at the center of the room. In other cases, only the best man and maid of honor, along with the couple's parents, will be seated at the bride's table, with the rest of the wedding party seated at a nearby table.

Often, newlyweds choose to sit on their own, at a table for two often referred to as the sweethearts' table, instead of having a bridal table. This makes it easier for them to circulate during the meal. (Some couples also do this to avoid having to exclude good friends who aren't in the wedding party from the high-status table.) In this situation, the wedding party will generally be seated together, near the bridal couple's table for two.

You'll know it's time for you to head to your seat when (a) the receiving line is finished and you see the bride and groom heading to their table, (b) someone gives a signal indicating that everyone should move to the dining area, or (c) you and the cutie you're talking to are suddenly the only people left at the pre-reception cocktail bar.

At the bride's table, the traditional seating arrangement is as follows: the maid of honor on the groom's left, the best man on the bride's right, with the other bridesmaids and ushers, and their significant others, on either side. Men and women usually alternate, and couples may be seated in a staggered manner, instead of next to each other, to mix things up and encourage socializing.

Sometimes, the spouses and significant others of the wedding party can't be included at the bridal table because of lack of space. If this is the case, the attendant, whether married or not, stays with the bridal party.

 ## FORMAL PHOTO TIPS

Professional photographers are part of almost every wedding, and so are what might seem like endless rounds of posed shots. Before you get grumpy, remember that the bride and groom are paying big bucks to have this shutterbug catch them and their loved ones on the big day. Deal with the wet grass, try your best not to squint, and smile until it hurts! This is what friendship is about.

The posed group photographs are usually taken after the ceremony, often at the reception site. Increasingly, however, couples are having them taken before the wedding, when everyone is at his or her most picture-perfect. Be sure you know when and where to show up with your smile.

As in any endurance activity, caffeine will enhance your performance—and after the first fifty photos, you'll be glad to have the help.

Don't shy away from using your best camera-ready skills to look fabulous in the photos—they will be preserved for years to come, after all. In group shots, angle your body toward the photographer and put one foot in front of the other like a celebrity on the red carpet. Lift your chin, pull back your shoulders, and keep your arms slightly tensed—in a sleeveless bridesmaid dress, pressing your arms flat against your sides always looks unflattering. During the reception, freshen your lipstick and powder frequently, and make sure your pearly whites look flawless—photographers usually stay at the party clicking away until the lights dim.

ALL ABOUT DANCING

Traditionally, the dancing begins after the first course and continues throughout the evening, although these days receptions differ greatly and there are many possible alternatives to this schedule. At some ceremonies, the music and dancing do not begin until after the meal is finished. With a traditional schedule, however, dancing will proceed as follows: First, the bride and groom dance together. Next, the parents join them on the dance floor—for example, the bride's father may cut in on the groom to dance with the bride, and then the groom may ask the bride's mother to dance. Then the bridal party is called to the dance floor and jumps into the mix—bridesmaids, dance with your groomsmen! After a few minutes, whoever is at the microphone will invite everyone onto the dance floor. Dancing, eating, and drinking will continue until it is time to cut the cake. Encourage guests to get up and dance! A packed dance floor will make the reception feel like a righteous party, and it will enable the bride and groom to leave the dance floor and mingle with other guests.

DEFENSIVE DANCING, OR HOW TO RECOGNIZE POTENTIALLY DANGEROUS PARTNERS

Whether you have to pair up with a clumsy groomsman or oblige the bride's buttoned-up cousin when he asks for a dance, what goes down on the reception dance floor isn't always pretty. The truth is, men stopped being trained in formal ballroom dancing quite a while ago, and most women naturally dance better than most (straight) men. Plus, in your extra-special bridesmaid's outfit, you are easily recognizable and approachable, and many male guests will feel comfortable asking you to dance, simply because you are wearing The Dress. Being a bridesmaid doesn't mean you must partner up with everyone who asks, but the festive reception spirit will probably persuade you to take a twirl with folks you wouldn't pick out of the lineup on your own. The best way to avoiding dance floor disasters? Gauge his dancing before you grab his hand. Study up on these classifications so you know what to expect when you join him on the dance floor.

* **The Geek:** What he lacks in rhythm, he makes up for with enthusiasm—just don't expect this dorky dude to help you look graceful. On the upside? His lack of self-consciousness should inspire you to have a great time no matter what.

* **The Fumbler:** Off the dance floor, he's an average man wearing an unremarkable suit. He is difficult to spot until you see his moves—but by then it's too late, and you're just inches away from him, trying to sway to the music. He will probably be grateful if, after one song, you suggest heading to the bar for a refreshing drink.

* **The Lover:** Be sure you're ready for his hip-grinding style when you agree to be his partner—shy girls might want to steer clear. This guy's sexy moves draw the spotlight every time!

* **The Swinger:** He'll whip you around in twirls and dips that might make the room do the same—especially if you've downed a bit too much cake and champagne. If you have a strong stomach and enjoy a strong lead, however, some fast turns on the floor with this mover and shaker are good for a rush!

* **The Waltzer:** Follow his steps, and concentrate. The waltz is supposed to be easy, but usually it's the old guys who bring out these moves, so just remember: Your misstep could land him in the ER.

 ## THE BOUQUET TOSS

After the dancing, it's usually time for the ceremonial cutting of the wedding cake, where the bride and groom feed each other. Then, the bride gathers her bridesmaids for the bouquet toss, if one will take place. Setting up the bridesmaids and other single female guests to jostle and shove to be the "lucky" one to catch the flowers—the sign that they will be married next—is

a tradition that seems to endure. But the toss inspires less fervor now than it did back when single women over thirty were called spinsters. No matter what your feelings are on the issue, however, every unmarried bridesmaid should participate in the toss. Get into it! And, if the bouquet comes toward you, do not run away.

If a garter toss will take place, it happens after the bouquet toss. The groom tosses the bride's garter to the bachelors (he might remove it from the bride's leg directly beforehand, in front of the crowd). According to tradition, the man who catches it will be the next to get married. At some weddings, the man who catches the garter is asked to put it on the leg of the woman who catches the bouquet. This situation has potential to become a completely embarrassing disaster for everyone involved, but you never know—if sparks fly between the two, a romance might take root.

Spectacular Speeches and Triumphant Toasts

The toasts usually begin once the champagne glasses are filled and the first course is served. Traditionally, the best man rises first to toast to the couple and follows with a speech that teases the groom and goes for laughs. Maid of honor, you're next in line. The bride and groom might then stand and thank everyone for coming, with family members or other friends who wish to say a few words taking their turns afterward. At a very casual wedding where the floor is opened for speeches, one member of the couple might receive more toasts than the other. If you notice the scales tipping in the bride's or the groom's favor, and you aren't otherwise scheduled to speak, jump up and honor the less toasted individual.

If you know in advance that you will be giving a speech, don't wait until the last minute to come up with ideas. Recognize the importance of planning ahead and use our Toasting Tips to bring the house down.

 ## TOASTING TIPS

Think of it this way: That wedding crowd will applaud no matter what you say. Okay—your toast should definitely honor the bride and groom—but the point is that you shouldn't feel compelled to be supremely witty, romantic, clever, poetic, or anything else that doesn't come naturally. Keeping your voice steady and standing up straight (without fidgeting) in front of a crowd is difficult enough, but it gets even harder if you don't feel totally comfortable with the content of your speech. Being confident is arguably the most important part of public speaking—so if you enjoy being funny, by all means be funny—but if you want to be serious, that's fine, too.

If you are the maid of honor, you may give a speech at the rehearsal dinner and at the wedding reception. The bride will usually give you advance warning if she expects you to speak at the reception. Bridesmaids who wish to make a toast generally do so at the rehearsal dinner, although, depending on the bride's wishes and the reception schedule, they may also do so at the wedding.

Making a wonderful, touching, and entertaining toast takes work. Speaking on the spur of the moment may sound great during those weeks of procrastination before the wedding, but the stress you'll experience as the time gets closer just isn't worth it. Besides, speeches given without some advance preparation often seem to ramble. The best way to alleviate your anxiety is to brainstorm ideas early, and practice in private. Follow these practical tips to deliver an unforgettable toast.

✳ Contextualize your connection to the bride. Without getting into boring details, mention how long you've known her, how you met, and some significant detail of your friendship.

✳ Touch on why you love her so much, what makes her special, and why you feel honored to be speaking at her wedding.

✳ Compliment the groom. If you know him well, this should be easy. If you don't know him well, focus on his accomplishments: "Leave it to Stacy to find a man who went to culinary school, can fix any problem on a car, and serenades her with his guitar at night." You can also talk about the ways he makes her happy. If you're at a loss, ask the bride for her ideas—she should be able to supply them in abundance, and at least a couple of them should be tame enough for family to hear.

✳ Wish them a long and happy life together.

✳ Be heartfelt but not long-winded.

✳ Do some research. If you can't find the right words, find a poem or quote that expresses your feelings for you.

✳ Don't fidget. Hold the microphone with one hand and keep the other one at your side, until it is time to pick up your glass to toast the couple.

✳ Visualize the situation in advance. Will you be speaking to forty people or four hundred? Will you be standing on stage with a microphone, or speaking from your assigned table? Having a good idea of the particulars will help you avoid bridesmaid-in-the-headlights syndrome. Don't worry about memorizing every last word of the speech—using notes is perfectly acceptable as long as you also make eye contact with the crowd.

✳ After you put down the microphone and head back to your seat, don't denigrate your speech by making negative comments about it afterward, even if your voice was shaking or you forgot part of it and ad-libbed badly. The point is not to draw attention to yourself, but to celebrate your friend and try your best. You'll probably be surprised by just how touched the bride and the guests are by your speech, even if you don't feel like you aced it.

✳ **Note:** Since rehearsal dinners are generally more intimate and casual than weddings, bridesmaids sometimes take the opportunity to do something more elaborate than a toast, such as getting together to perform a hilarious skit, or giving a slide show of the bride and groom as kids. Be sure the hosts are amenable before you plan something creative.

❗ THE WORD ALERT:
THE TOPPER

This word is sometimes used to describe something that puts a cap on a situation, such as, "It's bad enough that I was singing the *Burlesque* soundtrack in public, but faking a striptease—now that was the topper!" At weddings, however, the term refers to the miniature bride-and-groom figurine that goes on the wedding cake. ✳ **USAGE:** The bride says, ***"We paid the caterer four hundred bucks to find us that fabulous vintage topper."*** Correct response: ***"Now that's the topper."***

Doing Damage Control: How to Handle Other People's Bad Behavior

Weddings, like holidays, wouldn't be true celebrations without a little bad behavior. This is no reflection on the bride or groom, but simply a fact of life: People misbehave at weddings. Prepare yourself for the worst by acquainting yourself with some of the most common types of poor behavior—and learn exactly how to respond in the fashion most befitting a fabulous bridesmaid.

THE DYSFUNCTIONAL DRAMA!

The recent divorce between the bride's parents is making things tense. The groom's father brought his latest floozy girlfriend to the ceremony, and the groom's mother is offended. The bride's older sister just announced her divorce the day before the ceremony. Let's face it: Weddings are supposed to be about families coming together in the name of love, but sometimes the love just isn't there, and every conceivable moment feels potentially explosive.

▶ *Be prepared:* **Smile constantly, and defuse dangerous conversations by introducing totally neutral topics. For example, "Doesn't the wedding cake look lovely?"**

THE ME! ME! ME!

A family member or friend gives a self-referential toast that barely refers to the bride and groom, for example, "Marriage makes me think of my ex-spouse/coming out/ first love affair." This is particularly likely to come from a "black sheep" in the family.

▶ *Be prepared to:* **Respond just as you would to anyone else's speech, by clapping or smiling or raising your glass—as long as everyone else** does it—even if the person's words seemed completely offensive to you. Don't speak your judgment aloud. It's impossible to know right away whether the relatives found the toast atrocious; behavior that some people find utterly shocking is perfectly acceptable to others.

THE WILD CHILD!

A willful kid is allowed to run amok at the reception because his or her parents are too busy partying (or making out in the garden) to rein in the child. This scene can cause near-fatal disruptions on the dance floor, distract from the ceremonial cake cutting, and generally disturb the bride's peace of mind.

Be prepared: **Locate the parents, but if they are unavailable, attempt to get the child under control without creating an unpleasant spectacle. Avoid disciplining the kid, unless you are prepared to incur the wrath of the parents, or, worse, babysit for the night.**

THE ELEPHANT IN THE ROOM!

Every single person in the bride's and groom's collected families studiously ignores the antics of the attending alcoholic, who everyone hoped desperately would behave but who is progressively becoming more obnoxious and drunk.

Be prepared: **Follow suit and ignore the situation or, in an emergency, such as buffet table about to be toppled, take action.**

Thanks to the excellent rules of etiquette, there's no need to lug a wedding present in your suitcase—you officially have up to a year after the wedding to send the gift! If the wedding expenses have depleted your bank account, this rule permits you to recover financially before choosing the gift.

Don't feel compelled to purchase something lavish—even if you know that the other bridesmaids are dropping a fortune. Aim to spend somewhere between $50 and $150. Remember that any heartfelt offering will be welcomed! Another excellent solution to financial woes is to go in on the wedding gift with others—buying something expensive and memorable is easier when several people share the cost. You may also choose to purchase a wedding gift off the registry. There is no excuse for neglecting to send your gift within the allotted year—ignore those false rumors that say bridesmaids are exempt from giving wedding gifts because of their previous expenditures, such as the dress. Even a small gift can show how much you care. For a traditional Jewish wedding, for example, you could give seven small, inexpensive gifts, each representing one of the seven traditional Jewish marriage blessings. Another option is to sew throw pillows, knit scarves for the couple, or create some special artwork—handcrafting the present will make it memorable.

For indecisive bridesmaids, a gift certificate provides the perfect solution—particularly when you are close to the bride but not as well acquainted with the groom. Dinner for two at their favorite restaurant, a pair of theater or sporting-event tickets, or an overnight stay at a romantic bed-and-breakfast gives the couple the opportunity for an intimate evening together.

After the Reception

After the bouquet toss and one last dance for the newlyweds, the reception usually draws to a close as the couple makes a grand exit with all the guests cheering and waving good-bye. But just because the official event is over doesn't mean the bridal party can head home and put up their feet—here's an overview of what to expect once the reception site lights have been dimmed.

THE SEND-OFF

Brides often rely on their bridesmaids to help create a special send-off from the reception. At the chosen time, the maid of honor and bridesmaids should get their supply of rose petals, confetti, bubbles, or sparklers—and distribute them to all the guests—so the assembled crowd can shower the newlyweds with tokens and good wishes as they leave. Most couples these days stick around at least for an after-party, but if the couple plans to depart on a honeymoon directly, the bride may also need her bridesmaids' help changing out of her bridal gown and preparing to leave.

*...times, a maid of honor or bridesmaid goes above and beyond in
...ping with practical details after the reception—here are a few special
ways to lend a hand.*

✱ Make yourself generally available after the bride and groom depart the
reception, and ask key players like the bride's mother how you can help.
You can offer to collect the cake topper, the top tier of the wedding cake,
the guest book, extra flowers, and wedding gifts, and transport them to
a designated place. Usually, the best man or the bride's father will be in
charge of tipping the musicians and caterers, but you can always add your
enthusiastic thanks.

✱ Take charge of the bride's gown after the wedding, arranging for
cleaning and/or storage in a safe place until she returns from her
honeymoon. If you make the offer, here are some helpful hints: (a) have
the box or bag the dress arrived in on hand so you have a safe vessel
for transport; (b) read the small print, and if a cleaner asks you to sign
a disclaimer releasing them from responsibility
for damage to the dress, look for another, more
reputable service; (c) ask whether
they use acid-free packing materials
and boxes—this should be standard
practice for a wedding-dress cleaner.

✱ If the bride opted to supply
guests with disposable cameras—
yes, despite the digital revolution,
these remain a popular reception
staple and even come in tons
of colorful styles to match

table décor—offer to collect them and develop the prints. Even if the professional wedding photographs are digital, they won't be available immediately, so piles of fun snapshots provide the newlyweds with instant memories they can't get elsewhere.

THE AFTER-PARTY

In the old days, the end of the reception was the end of the wedding festivities—but today, that isn't always the case. An after-party where the newlyweds can unwind with close friends after the day's big events is now a popular tradition. The event might be a super casual gathering at a pub near the reception site where everyone pays for their own drinks, a spontaneous get-together in someone's hotel suite, or a more organized event with a DJ and an open bar. No matter what type of party it is, and even if you feel ready to crawl into bed, making an appearance is the right thing to do.

DAY-AFTER BRUNCH

Newlyweds often stick around the day after the wedding for a late morning or midday event that includes close family, the wedding party, and other guests who may not be flying out until later in the day. It might be a casual brunch at a nearby restaurant or the home of a friend or family member; or, in warm weather, an outdoor picnic or beach barbecue. Traditionally, such occasions have been organized by the bride's mother, but these days, anyone with the inclination or means may host the event. If you have stayed up partying all night and morning brunch is the last thing on your mind—with the possible exception of a burn-your-bridesmaid-dress party—simply show up briefly with a smile on your face and offer your warmest thanks and congratulations to the newlyweds and their families.

Fabulous Ways to Revive Yourself after Being a Bridesmaid

✳ Put on your crafting hat (okay, or find a seamstress) and turn those yards of high-end dress fabric into some stylish new throw pillows.

✳ Treat yourself to some lovely aromatherapy candles, indulgent new silky pajamas, and an afternoon massage. Why should you only overspend on other people?

✳ Host a bad bridesmaid dress fashion show—at home, behind closed doors, with no married friends invited. The guest who wears the most unflattering bridesmaid dress, and has the pictures to prove she wore it in public, wins a gift! (Have everyone chip in ten bucks for a gift certificate to a salon, so the lucky winner can have the beauty that she deserves.)

✳ Start a company that designs bridesmaid dresses that are affordable and flattering, and watch your net worth soar.

✳ Use your bridesmaid experience as a cocktail party conversation starter. You'll be amazed at how the shiest wallflowers or deafest old folks will perk up when this topic arises. When you feel really confident with your material, consider starting a podcast or a television talk show!

✳ Write a book about your bridesmaid experience.

✳ Schedule celebratory drinks with the bride—well, she's not really a bride anymore, is she?—and tell her how delighted you are to have her joining you back on Earth.

Resources

Bridesmaid Dresses

Ann Taylor Wedding
www.anntaylor.com
Seasonally changing collections of bridesmaid dresses

BHLDN
www.bhldn.com
Bridesmaid frocks from Anthropologie's wedding line

David's Bridal
www.davidsbridal.com
National wedding chain with huge selection of bridesmaid styles, sizes, and prices

The Dessy Group
www.dessy.com
Appealing and extensive collection of designer lines at all price levels; source of free Pantone chips for matching color to bridesmaid gowns

J. Crew Wedding
www.jcrew.com
Seasonally changing collections of bridesmaid dresses

Two Birds
www.twobirdsbrides maid.com
Hip bridesmaid styles with a specialty in convertible dresses

Bridesmaid Dress Alterations

WeddingWire
www.weddingwire.com
Search by zip code to find gown alterations experts nearby and reviews of their work (wedding vendors only)

Yelp
www.yelp.com
Search by zip code to find tailors nearby and reviews of their work (not wedding specific)

Bridal Blogs and Message Boards

100 Layer Cake
www.100layercake.com
Craft projects, vendor resources, and online marketplace to buy and sell wedding items

Bride to Bride
www.bridetobride boutique.com
Resale site for wedding-related items ranging from confetti to cake charms, jewelry to handbags

The Knot
www.theknot.com
Highly trafficked message boards where brides connect and advise each other

Once Wed
www.oncewed.com
Hundreds of inspirational bridesmaid images from real weddings; go-to site for used wedding gowns 25 to 50 percent off the retail price

Style Me Pretty
www.stylemepretty.com
Style-savvy wedding resource with an emphasis on chic DIY projects

Weddingbee
www.weddingbee.com
Highly trafficked message boards; "Month Twins" connect brides getting married the same time of year

Event Planning

Doodle
www.doodle.com
Easy online tool for event scheduling

Bridal Shower and Bachelorette Invitations

Chronicle Books
www.chroniclebooks.com/
bridesmaidguide
Downloadable templates for invitations, games, and party accessories

Paper Source
www.paper-source.com
Decorative papers, envelopes, rubber stamps, and more

Wedding Paper Divas
www.weddingpaperdivas.com
Stylish paper invitations for showers and parties

Favors, Décor, and Gifts

Bayley's Boxes
www.bayleysboxes.com
Distinctive gift packaging including pyramid boxes, and box bouquets

Etsy
www.etsy.com
One-of-a-kind wedding or shower gifts, unique décor items, and gift packaging Suggested sellers:

• *Simply VS (unique die-cut favor boxes including a wedding dress style)*
• *The Gilded Bee (charming handmade tags, labels, and trims)*

MOO
us.moo.com
Create stickers and cards using your own images

Save on Crafts
www.save-on-crafts.com
Bridal shower–themed décor such as white tulle plus DIY favor kits

Shutterfly
www.shutterfly.com
Create digital photo books using your own images

Sophie's Favors
www.sophiesfavors.com
Fun shower favors of all sorts with personalization available

Zingerman's
www.zingermans.com
Gourmet purveyor for food-themed shower favors or group gifts for the bride

Electronic Invitations
Evite
www.evite.com
The familiar electronic invitation service

Paperless Post
www.paperlesspost.com
Stylish electronic invitations

Bachelorette Party Accessories
Amazon
www.amazon.com
• *The Bachelorette Party Kit: box set with tiara, temporary tattoos, and games*
• *Bachelorette Party Lotto: scratch-off dares*

Babeland
www.babeland.com
Sex toys and romantic gift kits

Beau-coup
www.beau-coup.com
Fun, affordable bachelorette favors

Making Memories & More
www.makingmemoriesandmore.net
Rhinestone bridal party tees, sashes, veils

Budget Travel and Airfare
Craigslist
www.craigslist.org
Online communities featuring free classified advertisements including sections devoted to vacation rentals and apartment swaps

Hotwire
www.hotwire.com
Deep discounts on hotels and car rentals

Kayak
www.kayak.com
Comprehensive search engine for travel

Priceline
www.priceline.com
Discounts on hotels and car rentals

Southwest
www.southwest.com
Affordable plane fares and car rentals

Zipcar
www.zipcar.com
Car-sharing service

Miscellaneous
Victoria's Secret
www.victoriassecret.com
Replacement straps for convertible bras and all types of underpinnings

WhatSheBuys
www.whatshebuys.com
Free same-day shipping on Spanx and other underpinnings

YouTube
www.youtube.com
Online beauty tutorials

Zappos
www.zappos.com
Huge shoe selection with free shipping and returns

Index

LET THE GAMES BEGIN!

This little booklet will guarantee the bride-to-be a night she'll never forget. Each scratch-off card includes a sassy set of dares for the bachelorette and her bridesmaids to complete throughout the evening. And as an added bonus, a collection of sexy temporary tattoos lets everyone know who's ready to party.

CHRONICLE BOOKS